THE STRANGE LETTER Z

THE
STRANGE
LETTER
Z

Debra Daley

BLOOMSBURY

For Chad

First published in Great Britain 1996
Copyright © 1995 by Debra Daley

The moral right of the author has been asserted

Bloomsbury Publishing Plc, 2 Soho Square, London W1V 6HB

A CIP catalogue record for this book
is available from the British Library

ISBN 0 7475 2305 3

10   9 8 7 6 5 4 3 2 1

Typeset by Hewer Text Composition Services, Edinburgh
Printed in Great Britain by Clays Ltd, St Ives Plc

ACKNOWLEDGEMENTS

The author gratefully acknowledges the assistance of the Literature Programme of the Arts Council of New Zealand Toi Aotearoa.

In writing this novel, I have drawn on the work of many linguists and anthropologists, particularly Evon Z. Vogt's – and his students' – studies of the Zinacantecos of Mexico. The character of Samuel Zeugen was provoked by the life and work of Edward Sapir, especially his writing about 'drift' and 'spirit', although the details in this novel diverge from actuality. Alexis's automatic exposition of d'Alembert's 'general system of the sciences and the arts' derives from a translation of the 1751 *Discours préliminaire Encyclopédie* Paris: Briasson, David, Le Creton, Durand.

An extract from this novel appeared in *Landfall*, New Series, Vol. I, No. 2, Spring 1993, published by Oxford University Press (New Zealand).

Do you not discern in that letter Z an adverse influence? Does it not prefigure the wayward and fantastic progress of a storm-tossed life? . . . Marcas! Does it not hint of some precious object that is broken with a fall, with or without a crash?

Honoré de Balzac, Z. Marcas

1

When the school bus arrived at her unmarked stop, Nerida, motivated by the excitement of new stationery, leaped from the top step on to the soft grass verge of the highway. The stationery bounced around in her leather satchel as she sprinted up the long driveway leading to the kitchen of her family's farmhouse in Northland. She was a sensible seven year old whose smile was enlarged by the conviction that she would probably win the Standard 150-yard dash at the end of term, and that, of all the girls in her class, her ponytail was the longest. She also knew the farm by heart and had no reason to suppose that anything would ever change.

The Simmonds's wooden house, standing on an eminence, was painted mauve with a lemon trim in keeping with a national preference, which reached its zenith during the fifties, for high-keyed pastels; as if the owners of these candy-coloured houses, having led harsh or drab lives as children, were making a last stab at playfulness.

No matter what the season, Nerida thought as she approached her home, the surrounding trees were always trembling. She liked to watch shafts of light roam across country, illuminating the contours of the land. Green paddocks, sloping away beyond the house, were complicated by archipelagos of volcanic rock, intersected by drystone walls and wire fences, and bordered by four large ridged cones bearing the marks of pre-European settlements.

Nerida's parents, whom she loved, looked like all the other parents, the ones attached to her schoolfriends. The fathers, smelling of tobacco and agricultural products, went about with brutal haircuts and blunt hands abused by hard work. The mothers, smelling of cold cream and vegetables, buttoned thin nylon cardigans over their print dresses while their faces dried up in the sun which assailed them as they brought in the washing. These men and women were young, in their twenties, but they had surrendered their youth, suddenly, upon marrying. They embraced tradition. They became practical. When they looked into the sky they saw only weather and its effect on income.

Mrs Simmonds was standing, as ever, at the stove, engaged in a form of domesticity which her daughter did not consider to be unusual. While Nerida rocked back and forth dangerously on a modern kitchen chair, devouring gigantic after-school biscuits, farmers' wives the length and breadth of New Zealand were mixing scone dough or trimming a joint of mutton for roasting. But Mrs Simmonds was preparing comfits to sweeten the family's mouths at the end of a meal. Using a pair of tweezers, she dipped each aromatic seed, fennel, caraway and coriander which she had grown and dried herself, in a syrup of melted sugar and then allowed them to dry, spread out on mesh in a patch of November sunlight on the red formica bench. She was compelled to repeat the process again and again in order to coat the seeds with a sufficiently crunchy layer of sugar. The task took several days.

Nerida had finished her comic which was filled with competitions and special offers for Residents of the United Kingdom and Northern Ireland Only. Her mother was dipping the final layer. The kitchen was painted in what Mrs Simmonds described as cheerful colours which remained undimmed even when the sun disappeared as it did now.

2

Sudden rain slapped at the windows. Maybe it was all the yellow and red and blue or the scrupulous, intense labour at the bench, but Nerida felt, watching her mother, as though insects were crawling over her limbs. She bounded outside, on to the porch, and then stepped into the warm rain with her eyes closed.

On the road below, a car shrieked. Nerida opened her eyes to see a large vehicle slewing off the straight metal road. Leaping the ditch, it chewed up twenty yards of wire fence before keeling over beside the Simmonds's iron letter-box. Nerida ran to the woolshed to fetch her father, who was shearing, then he and the foreman helped a shaken American couple, tourists, from the car. As the squall passed on, heading east, birds began to sing. Droplets of leftover rain glittered in the trees.

After Mrs Simmonds had come belting down the drive in the truck to take the strangers to a doctor, Nerida found a magazine sprawled face down in the paddock, apparently flung there from the car. Its cover was almost detached from its spine. Carefully she picked up the magazine, an old copy of *Harpers Bazaar*, and carried it to her room where she repaired it with Sellotape. It was not the kind of magazine you ever saw in Northland. Its pages were rich with advertisements for fur coats and advanced furniture. When Mrs Simmonds returned in the early evening with the news that the Plymouth was to be towed away and that the Americans were on their way to Auckland, Nerida felt free to cut up the magazine. She transferred the pages to her previously bare walls.

For ten years, until the accident happened, resulting in her father's craziness and the loss of the farm, Nerida woke each morning and went to sleep each night with her gaze fixed on a certain illustration. The memory of it comforted her later when she was living with a succession of indifferent relatives. A woman looked away to her left, her eyes mysterious with

3

mascara, her mouth a smudge of lipstick. The photographed woman had been painted over with exciting brushstrokes. All the detail was burnt out of her, leaving a racy essence of movement. A large, blurry shadow hovered behind her. The picture was black-and-white except for a yellow smear indicating the coat. The woman was probably looking at someone to say, as Nerida did as she grew older and more churned-up, stretch me out just where I am here on this porch so boring I'd like to set it on fire and do something, whatever that thing is that this body is waiting for. Sometimes in the middle of the night, Nerida would take off her nightdress and step on to the wooden bed-end which bit into the soles of her feet, her arms outstretched for balance like a winged Victory. It made her shiver to think of her parents in the house, practically dead, while she was poised and elevated with the window open so that the breeze stole over her.

'I think your hair should be tidied up.' Mrs Simmonds, standing in the Curl Up & Dye Salon on the sun-blasted main street of Kaitaia, was squinting at her daughter. Nerida didn't say yes, and she didn't say no. So her ponytail was sheared off. Afterwards, as her mother extracted money from her purse to pay for the haircut, Nerida could not keep her eyes off the floor, where the junior was busy sweeping up her blonde hair. Nerida wanted to keep it. There were great hanks of hair being swept into the dustpan. But that was impossible. What would she do with it?

'You look much tidier,' said her mother as they drove back home. 'It's an improvement.'

The season was high summer, approaching the stickiness of February, and the haircut was in preparation for high-school. Nerida felt naked without the weight of her hair lying on her neck. She didn't understand why her mother had made her cut it. Meandering into the garden, Nerida found that the sweet peas had gone to seed, their contracted pods hardening into long, thin spirals. When she touched them lightly, her fingertips detonated the casing and the seeds exploded into her hand.

The years crawled by like some low-lying thing, some insinuating parasite, even though Mr and Mrs Simmonds had bought a television set as a distraction. Nerida watched it constantly, eventually neglecting her schoolwork in order to live in its flexible universes. They gradually replaced the reality of the farm, which had shrunk to a collection of inevitable chores and predictable meals. Mrs Simmonds had ceased to make comfits, although she did continue to garden intently. She lavished attention on her plants, especially the frangipani which she was training to climb up the north-facing side of the house outside Nerida's bedroom. She discussed it at tea-time and worried about it and borrowed books about it. The frangipani continued to grow and Nerida supposed that that was an achievement.

As Nerida sank deeper into adolescence, she was attacked by inexplicable anxieties which angered her parents. The vegetable garden behind the house, for instance. Although she liked eating asparagus, Nerida tried to avoid the bed because it filled her with horror to see the spears sticking up out of the dark soil like blind, green baby cobras. These beds were permanent. She was agitated by reports, usually only a paragraph or two tucked away inside the newspaper, of tragic events visited on ordinary unsuspecting citizens. Student killed in birthday car crash. Fisherman drowns trying to free bird. Festive drinks led to fall. And then to escape the habitual silences of her parents, she would run off with a magazine to a place she had made for herself, a cave she had excavated in a pocket of bush, not far from the fenced-in backyard. Nerida drew zigzags around the entrance to the cave to signify lightning bolts.

Even at the cave she could hear the blows coming from the garage. Her mother had embarked on an infuriating hobby. Other mothers pursued quiet recreations. They made rag rugs or dolls with voluminous skirts designed to fit over rolls of toilet paper. But Mrs Simmonds, inspired by a library book, had begun building and distressing furniture. Watching her mother reduce the corners of a chest with files and rasps made Nerida uneasy. She appreciated her mother's capacity for enthusiasm, but judged it often to be misdirected. In her heart Nerida believed that her mother might have expended her energies on an exclusive devotion to her daughter. Not those wooden constructions about which she had become passionate.

Mrs Simmonds would scar a chest, striking it with a hammer and chain, producing so much noise it was impossible to speak to her. When she progressed to the next stage, perhaps inserting a heated wire in the wood to simulate wormholes, she worked with a wilful concentration which also precluded communication. After this mutilation was complete, Mrs Simmonds would darken the object with walnut powder and orange shellac until its origins were completely obscured.

Mr Simmonds dipped sheep and fenced and said nothing about the chests and chairs and small tables now crowding the house.

Under the influence of a tentacular, brooding spectre called Self, Nerida slowly drifted apart from her friends who were already going out with beefy, freckled boys assigned to become their husbands. When Nerida observed these contented sixteen-year-old couples sharing meat pies and massive doughnuts at lunchtime, she could make no connection between this version of romance and the sickening inadmissable delirium that gripped her when she saw Stephen, one of her father's intermittent stockmen, unsaddling his horse, measuring out the feed, oiling the bridles. She could think of nothing to say to him apart from the occasional tight-lipped hello which effectively established her as an uppity bitch. In desperation she began spending her lunch hours reading non-fiction in the school library, trying to make up for all the years she had spent watching the kind of television that had encouraged her to become a girl who thought in such terms as 'sickening inadmissable delirium'. A bewildered girl afraid of banality who had scarcely passed School Certificate although she had once been clever.

On a stifling afternoon late in March, Nerida failed once more to strike up a conversation with Stephen. He was walking his horse through the gate while she was standing at the letter-box wondering whether or not to take off her cardigan. He nodded. He was wearing sunglasses, an outrageous affectation in a stockman. All that came into her head was a rush of random information about fruit gardens in Zeeland, and then her throat locked. She smiled horribly at him. She went to bed without eating, which caused an argument with her parents. Self-centred. Self-obsessed. Self-destructive. Later that night, unable to sleep, Nerida removed her nightdress and looked at herself in the mirror. Her body was the colour of watered milk; her breasts were made of silk. Touching her nipples, she felt ill with elation. The older you got, the more you were invaded by emotions. She could see now that it was necessary to fight back with facts. They neutralised the hazardous combinations of chemicals in your brain. Sixth-form physics. That was a cooling subject. Nerida turned from the mirror to the open window containing a square of black, blank night and thought about a time before electrons had bound with atomic nuclei. After which photons, energetic particles of light and other forms of electro-magnetic radiation were released from their bondage with matter. The smell of frangipani infiltrated her bedroom.

Placing her hands on her hips, she dug her fingernails hard into her flesh, making tiny red crescents. The universe was still dark but punctuated by starlight, which was the decaying fervour of the photons recorded by radio astronomers. It was the trace of high temperatures which had once existed. The mystery of her mother's state of mind was like that, like radiation, invisible but dangerous, its harmfulness taking some time to manifest itself.

Nerida lay down again without resuming her nightdress. She raised her arms over her head as an act of suspense or surrender, and then she must have dozed because she was flying through the air over Zeeland, over islands consisting of a number of smaller islands, over the Drowned Land of South Beveland. She woke up nervously. Z used to be the seventh letter. It was present in the Etruscan, Oscan and Umbrian alphabets. Although she had begun to read again, the information that lodged in her brain seemed to be useless at school. Teachers wrote in her margins: 'Off the Point; Digressive; Meaning?' There was nowhere for the information to go which was probably why she felt like bursting. And then there would be a flood. And irreparable damage.

To avoid future calamities the Dutch government had constructed large dams enclosing the sea channels. Stretching her hand between her legs, Nerida was surprised to find herself melting. Sugar and water warmed over a flame until it liquified. She shivered. A disaster, a flood, could have occurred in Zeeland at any time so they built dikes and bridges to hold back the threat of the sea. As a result, it became possible to drive directly from central Holland to islands which had previously been rather isolated. Nerida's fingers were slippery. She moved them in slow circles, throwing her legs wide apart, and felt fathomless.

Reaching a hot centre that incinerated thought, she pushed

harder, her hips undulating, faster, creating friction, unable to stop. Something was glittering in the darkness inside her, shimmering, as if all over the sky stars were flaring into pinpricks of light and then some kind of warm wind came howling up her legs. She was sweating and kicking around, the ridges in the sheet burning against her shoulder-blades. Her feet were arched like a dancer's. Then a sensation caused her body to cease, as if she had been shot. Heat poured over her, an unknown hand tipping hot liquid over her skin, encasing her in pleasure. Her hand was aching but she continued to massage herself, unwilling to leave that land, that rehearsal for love, and then a different, slower excitation rippled through her. What was it, what summed her up? A word slid into her mind which she had never heard spoken aloud because it caused distress and high feeling. Under cover of night it was chalked on the asphalt surrounding the girls' lavatories. Cunt. White letters on black. Self blown up big then extinguished. Finally, Nerida felt capable of sleep.

2

Most nights of his childhood, until he was sent away to boarding school at the age of thirteen, Alexis Serafin memorised a page of the dictionary to minimise the possibility of a word taking him by surprise. Even before he had much of a personal history, memory was his forte. His ability to memorise was encouraged by his father with whom he played a variety of word games designed to arouse Alexis's intelligence. Dr Serafin was generous with facts. Walking the calm, sleek streets of their wealthy neighbourhood with his father, Alexis learnt that the average temperature of the universe was once three degrees above zero. Rowing across Orakei Basin to visit one of Auckland's few aesthetes, Alexis's father mentioned that linguistics is a more elevated subject than psychology which operates from a base of statistics. Dr Serafin's assumption that Alexis possessed an adult mind filled the boy with a gasping sense of achievement, the sweaty, hard-won kind that belongs to marathon runners and mountaineers. He was sweating now, standing on the lawn in his togs while his parents were detained inside the house. He was immobilised by the thought that linguistics depends on the mathematics of separation. The sun shone in a cloudless sky, promising an uninhibited summer.

Alexis yelped as a gout of cold water splashed across his face. He opened his eyes to find his stern, admirable sister, also in her bathing suit, cooling him down. Drusilla was brilliant at distractions, although for some reason not yet available to Alexis, his parents more often than not described her actions as wicked. Hooting loudly, Alexis and Drusilla capered around the sprinkler, letting themselves be whipped by the whirling spray. The grass under their feet turned slippery, which encouraged pleasurable falls and uncontrolled skids in the direction of the potentially painful rosebeds. Alexis loved throwing himself around like this. He was nothing but a body, a physical sensation, leaving Drusilla to be the mastermind. Just as he felt a twinge of boredom with their game, Drusilla detached the sprinkler, and with one finger pinching the nozzle of the hose, increased the water pressure so that they could take turns trying to knock one another off balance. Their cries grew more shrill, like gulls scrapping over waterfront rubbish bins. Suddenly, with a pointed glance at the upper storey of the house, Drusilla hissed, 'For God's sake, Alexis! Calm down. You'll wake them up.'

'You started it!'

Drusilla dropped the hose which sprang once at her calves, then fell listlessly on the ground. Water puddled around her feet. Placing her hands on her hips, she shook her head and said, 'You get away with anything.'

Alexis was stung by this accusation. It was not his fault that he liked playing the dictionary game. Someone had to.

Briskly Drusilla twisted her hair and wrung it out. Flicking droplets of water at him, she said, 'I'm going over to Fiona's,' and then, climbing the fence, was gone. Alexis surveyed the messed-up lawn. Drusilla was right. He wouldn't be blamed for it. He was the favourite and she was free to be furious.

A fortnight before his eleventh birthday, Alexis came down from his room to find his mother arranging lunch on the wide veranda.

'Hello, sweet boy,' Mrs Serafin murmured, and kissed

11

Alexis's cheek while glancing at her watch. Dr Serafin was expected home within the hour. Salami and slices of smoked beef, salads and dips glistened under the net she had spread to protect the food from flies. There was also a passionfruit cake. Pouring herself a glass of cold white wine, Mrs Serafin sipped it as she paced about the veranda, regarding the laden table critically.

'I think you could chuck the roses, Alexis. They don't look right. Too much like a restaurant. It's important not to convey the impression that you've gone to too much trouble.' You can care, but not too much.

Eager to participate in the preparations for his father's return, Alexis removed the vase of hybrids anchoring the net. When he returned from the kitchen, Mrs Serafin was reclining on the squeaking cane sofa, apparently satisfied with her scene-setting. Alexis stood on one leg with the other tucked up hard against his backside. 'Look, Mama, I've been amputated.'

His mother laughed and began stroking her velvet skirt so that the nap lay alternately dark and light. Mrs Serafin wore velvet in summer and chiffon in winter if she felt like it. Alexis realised that that kind of defiance was rare in the mothers he came across. Sometimes a woman would say to his mother, 'Aren't you hot, Caroline, in that dress?' And his mother would reply, 'Yes, I am. I enjoy a certain amount of discomfort.'

Her clothes, her style, marked her as emphatically alien in the same way that his Middle European accent marked Dr Serafin, causing the parents of Alexis's schoolfriends to refer to his family as immigrants. Actually, *émigrés*, Alexis always silently corrected. *Émigré* was a word that better suggested the atmosphere of distinction that clung to his parents. It was typical, he thought, of their adventurousness, that they had come to live in New Zealand, even though the

12

entire world lay at their feet. His father was a matchless asset to the university. His father's scholarship would place the university on the map. His father would arrange for Alexis to attend university in England so that Alexis could bathe in a comfortable future, which he would share with Drusilla.

Alexis dashed across the lawn and climbed on to the ivy-covered rock wall which terminated his parents' property. From this vantage point he viewed the multiflorous garden, the large, white wedding-cake of a house, the stagey veranda, the white tablecloth, the white clematis, and his mother very still, sheltered from the hot sun, wearing sunglasses against the glare. He was torn between his desire to remain on the wall where he could confirm at a distance the perfection of his precious home; and running back to the security of the veranda where he had no sense of perspective, where his mother would push the hair out of his eyes with fingers refreshingly chilled by the wineglass.

At the hum of an approaching car, Mrs Serafin rose to her feet. A blue Jaguar nosed into the driveway. Waving, Alexis sprang from the wall. The ratcheting sound of Dr Serafin pulling on the handbrake was a relief. His killing the engine was a relief: that meant he was home. Alexis galloped towards the Jaguar, accompanying himself with retroflex and buccal clicks.

After lunch, Dr Serafin brought from inside the house a glass of vodka and a dictionary. Unusually, a pang of resistance pricked at Alexis, lying warm and lazy on the smooth boards of the veranda.

'I feel sleepy,' he said to his mother, who was writing a letter to Drusilla. Drusilla had accompanied her father to Wellington, but was to remain there for a further fortnight. She was reluctantly on holiday, packed off to the home of a Czech acquaintance of Alexis's parents, whose daughter was the same age as Drusilla. Alexis expected that Drusilla would pretty soon mince up the Wellington girl. He felt lonely without his sister.

But Mrs Serafin did not reprieve her son. 'Sit up at the table with Papa,' she said. 'You know you both love to play.'

Alexis sat opposite his father and then, eyeing the dictionary, experienced a familiar leap of the heart. He could never tell how exacting the test would be, but if he acquitted himself well everything around him grew brighter, more ardent. Dr Serafin let the pages flutter through his fingers until the volume slumped open at 'Mappemond to March'.

'Let's see. Thirty-five principal words. Mappemond.'

'Mappemond. A noun. Historically a map of the world. And its obsolete meaning is the world itself. From the Low Latin, *mappa mundi*.'

A year earlier, Dr Serafin had introduced his son to transformational grammar, although leaving his wife to oversee the actual exercises. For example, surface structure: heavenly father. Deep structure: father, who is heavenly.

'Maquette.' Dr Serafin lit a Balkan Sobranie, waving the match languidly in the air so that the tiny flame took some time to die. He smoked delicately, holding the cigarette between his thumb and forefinger, as foreigners did.

'Maquette. A noun. A kind of – a model made of clay or wax of a piece of sculpture. From the French.'

'Maqui. M-a-q-u-i.' Dr Serafin leaned to his left and placed the cigarette between his wife's lips. She inhaled and then exhaled a cloud of aromatic smoke. While she did this, she looked into her husband's eyes, appraising him. He adjusted his glasses.

'Maqui. Noun. South American shrub.' Alexis did not care for the silent language of glances and gestures practised by his parents. How long did it take to become fluent in that language? Its rules were obscure and capricious. 'A South

American . . . evergreen shrub, which . . .' Forests of tree diagrams had proliferated in Alexis's notebooks. He loved the sentence S, the primitive, original whole which he thought of as a blue curving line like those he used to paint across the top of a page, when he was young, to mean SKY. The sentence S, which started at the top, contained all the operations necessary for the phonological and semantic to take effect. Then it descended, plunging through the trees, slipping down their branches towards the lower levels, towards the roots, into the ground where there were dark caves and sinkholes. Alexis had lost the thread.

'Yes?' Dr Serafin tilted his head to indicate his surprise at Alexis's faltering.

'Maqui. A noun. Its leaves . . . the leaves of the maqui . . . the green leaves of the maqui . . .'

'You have lost your concentration, Alexis. You are thinking about more than one thing at a time. That is good if your thought process is additive and combinatorial. The daydream is not so good. Watch out for that cul-de-sac.'

'Really, Antonin. Don't be such a stick.' Mrs Serafin spoke with a smile on her face, but this was just a decoy. Her tone suggested that she was fully armed, ready for combat. Alexis fidgeted at the table, flicking his gaze cautiously from one parent to the other. Some meaning was present in the deep structure which he could not decipher. It is true, very true, extremely true, he said to himself, that no system remains static. Opinions may alter. For instance, after he had spent a few months mastering transformational grammar, his father had declared that its transformational rules were riddled with absurdities. Dr Serafin had never trusted the intuitiveness of transformations and was not afraid to say so in print. He advised Alexis that in a few years' time he expected this school of grammar to be degraded by neurolinguistic therapists. Subject dismissed. Nothing is certain. Certainly

15

not consistent, except for rules of grammar, upon which one must rely.

Dr Serafin returned his wife's smile, then raised his arms in the air as if he were balancing a large, unstable object. 'Your mother has an artistic temperament, Alexis, for which we should be grateful. Of course the mind should exercise itself occasionally in fantasy and that sort of thing, but we don't want to be aimless, do we? The world is full of intelligent, perceptive people who have no idea how properly to employ their talents.' He shrugged, letting his hands collapse on to the table. 'Then they become depressed.'

Mrs Serafin reached for her wineglass, but finding it empty, bent once more over her letter. Keen to avoid aimlessness, Alexis concentrated hard on the subject of South American shrubs. There was a connection with his mother, her cool lips on his cheek . . . but before he could pin down the thought, his father supplied the missing definition.

'The berries of the maqui yield a medicinal wine. Maquillage.'

'Noun. The art of using make-up. French.' That was easy. Anything to do with the ornamentation of women was easy and usually sweet-smelling.

'Maquis. M-a-q-u-i-s.'

'Noun. French. Mediterranean, particularly Corsican, shrubbery. Thickets of shrubbery. And member of the maquis. French guerrilla band, Second World War.'

'Very good. Mar.'

Often the blandest words were the most demanding. Keep, long, new, pull, ring, take, well. And you could never tell about the character of a page. 'Mappemond to March', for example, involved a lot of recalcitrant botanical material. Already two shrubs had made an appearance. Alexis frowned at his face reflected in the polished surface of the silver tea-pot, whose curvature made him look grotesque. Mama

16

had always assured him that he was a handsome boy. You're beautifully shaped, she had said, more than once. What was more important? To play the dictionary game well, or to be a gorgeous boy, a candidate for caresses? It was so nice to be touched. And it was so nice to be approved of.

'Mar. Transitive verb. From old English merran. To damage, spoil.'

'Obsolete meaning?'

'To interfere with.'

'Two words derived from mar.'

'Marplot. Adjective and transitive verb. To defeat a plot by unwarranted interference. Martext. Adjective and intransitive verb. An ignorant preacher.'

But then Alexis began to think independently and his form declined. Philosophers, he said to himself while his father sipped at his vodka, waiting, are not so numerous as poets. The poets have the right to consider themselves above philosophers (Lautréamont); for there is no reason why here rather than there, why now rather than then (Pascal); I'm never never going to go to the stupid university (Drusilla); be sweet, be calm, darling boy, excuse me while I attend to your father (Mama); starlight is the decaying fervour of high temperatures that once existed (sixth-form textbook); our family name was once Zerafin but Papa changed it when he adopted English because the Z looks too foreign, it draws attention to itself although it once occupied a safe place in the alphabet surrounded by other letters until it reached Modern Times as defined by the Romans who were famous for being great engineers and debauchers, whatever the latter is in actuality, although I understand the word semantically. In mathematics Z denotes the third unknown quantity and there is something about this in Wittgenstein but I can't follow it. The idea of Wittgenstein makes me feel suddenly sad because I am almost eleven years old and I can't understand

17

Wittgenstein. All my friends are at the beach today. They are at Takapuna playing volleyball which is senseless but fun. Where has this melancholy come from? I must strike it from the record I'd like another slice of that passionfruit cake. Otherwise I'll become aimless and depressed like artists suffering from psychology. I won't succumb. I didn't when I was sick with that brain-fever and they thought I might die but I bounced back because I didn't really care about anything, not even death. (Alexis)

He missed three more plants, maranta, marattia and Marcgravia, the last an epiphytic shrub with pitcher-like bracts developed as nectaries. Visited by bloody humming birds.

Dr Serafin ground his cigarette into the ashtray. 'Thirty-one out of thirty-five is not bad.' He pressed a non-committal kiss on to his son's forehead. 'Now you can run off and play. Your mother and I want to talk.' But they didn't talk. They went upstairs and closed the door. They were the pattern of glamour, a glamour that Alexis wanted to obtain for himself. Its essential elements were beauty and distance. Alexis lounged once more on the rock wall, watching the house, wishing his sister were with him.

3

Nerida's family had been cruising along its programmed course as all ordinary families do, encapsulated by routine and here-and-now tasks which deflected attention from the enormity of life. However as another summer expired, Mrs Simmonds, it seemed to Nerida, had made a disconcerting sortie into outer space. Suddenly she was outside the mother-craft, attached to it only by a thin line, tumbling around in the void. Nerida watched her mother through the portholes, running gloved hands over the surface of the craft, searching for hairline cracks and other signs of material fatigue, and thought: She's spending an awfully long time out there. At home Mrs Simmonds continued making the beds and running the baths and plaiting Nerida's hair but she performed this maintenance in a vacuum which Nerida's overheated imagination rushed to fill with extreme images. Sometimes she anticipated, upon opening a door, finding her mother dangling from a noose or slumped across her blue bed, an empty tranquilliser vial at her side. This fear was, she told herself, ridiculous, because there was nothing in Mrs Simmonds's character to indicate a potential suicide. She'd ordered perennials for a spring planting. She'd had her hair permed in town. She'd ceased making furniture. There was nothing Nerida could put her finger on to explain the nervous atmosphere.

Early in April, Nerida dressed in a skirt printed with a

pattern of *Rosa centifolia* and eager to do anything at all to assuage her restlessness, made her way to the disintegrating cave that needed repairing. But as she came through the gate, she was mortified to encounter Stephen eating his lunch. He was chewing a large sandwich while turning the pages of a book that lay in his lap. Nerida froze. Stephen glanced up at her and smiled hello. Impatient of the wild emotions which always attacked her at the sight of him, Nerida incited herself to act normally.

'What's that book?' she demanded, adopting the voice her school principal employed when he accused certain pupils at assembly of delinquent behaviour.

Stephen met her gaze without speaking to show he did not care for her tone, then held the book up high so that she could see the botanical drawings. His face struck her as painfully intelligent. Carelessly Nerida took the volume from him and as she did so, accidentally touched his hand. She dropped the book in the soft earth, then knelt down and elaborately picked it up and offered it to him, with her face turned away as if she had noticed something fascinating in the adjacent empty paddock. Ignoring the book, he began to brush the mud off her skirt. His brown hair had a reddish cast to it. The muscles of his shoulder moved beneath his shirt as he flicked at her skirt.

'You can look at it if you want,' he said. 'It's about sub-tropical plants. Hoyas and cycads. I know you like books. I've seen you reading up a storm. You get tired of TV, I reckon. It's a downer.'

Believing these sentences to be the most intimate that anyone had ever said to her, Nerida stared at him with glazed eyes and open mouth. She might have pitched forward right then into his lap so that she could press her face against his stomach, so that she could say 'I love you', a phrase she had heard uttered frequently on television; but then Stephen added, 'I'd lend it to you except your old man's given me the boot. I'm off at the end of the week. That's a shame, eh.'

Nerida ran up the path towards the house, screaming internally. Someone had left the wheelbarrow on the lawn. A sickle glinted on top of its cargo of weeds. Nerida made for it, her hand closing on the smooth wooden handle, warm from the sun. The nerve-endings in her fingers conspired to send a great surge of energy through her body, climaxing in an instruction to her brain which was already primed by disappointment and frustration to act like a hooligan.

Nerida slashed at the frangipani. She hacked branches from the main stem, the sickle blade glancing off the weatherboarded wall, and was gratified by the fall of leaves and flowers and laterals. She chopped and cleaved, dramatically, as a seventeen year old does. She hated the tension in the kitchen in the evening when her father came in for tea. The abysmal gaps between observations about the weather or requests for tomato sauce or salt were explained by the sweeping phrase: 'bad mood'. Your mother's in a bad mood. Your father's in a bad mood. Nerida's in a mood. It didn't mean anything and yet everything appeared fraught with significance as if her family spoke an odd, terse language whose grammar was so highly inflected it could communicate an endemic sadness without actually making a direct statement. Nerida's parents had intimated that, when she left school at the end of the year, she was not to go to the city. They did not want her to go and there had been no further explanation. Her father had banished Stephen just when it seemed that he and Nerida could have had a conversation.

Nerida replaced the sickle in the wheelbarrow and fled to her room. With relief she heard the sound of Stephen's truck disappearing down the driveway. Gone, and just as well. Not likely to discover that she had been a stupid girl. For at least an hour Nerida's vandalism lay undiscovered, but in the moment

21

that guilt had convinced her to clean up the mess, she observed her mother passing by the bedroom window, lugging the ladder. Nerida began brushing her hair, looking towards the woman on the wall, who, as usual, was gazing elsewhere.

The sun had retreated and rain clouds were bowling across the sky from the west as Nerida slowly approached the scene of destruction. Her mother was halfway up the ladder, with garden twine in one hand, examining the damaged frangipani. Nerida hoped that she would say it didn't matter; that autumn was perfect for pruning and clearing away dead wood. But the staccato, offended movements of Mrs Simmonds's hands as they tied the ravaged plant back into place, and the rigid set of her face in profile, warned Nerida that her mother considered this a personal attack: a very bad example of Nerida's destructive emotions that would only reinforce the understanding that she was too unstable to be released into the world. Reaching for a branch that hung half-severed from the main stem, Mrs Simmonds raised her sandalled foot to step up another rung.

'I'm sorry! It was my fault!'

Mrs Simmonds turned sharply at the sound of Nerida's voice and then missed her footing and was suddenly falling backwards. In mid-air she flung out a hand, futilely, to save herself, and the ball of string dived towards the ground. She landed in a heap, mostly on her back, her head striking the concrete path, where the green twine was strung out like dyslexic scribble. The ladder remained upright.

'Mum!' Nerida crouched over her mother. Mrs Simmonds's eyes were closed, her face pale, older. Nerida touched her mother's cheek, uncomfortable with this familiarity, but pleased to see that her mother's hair-clips were still in place. Slowly Mrs Simmonds opened her eyes and stared for a second, puzzled, at Nerida.

'Blacked out,' she said.

Nerida slid her arm around her mother's shoulders and clumsily helped her up. Mrs Simmonds lightly touched the back of her head, wincing.

'Should I ask Dad to call Dr Farris?'

'No need. Bit of a rotten headache. Cup of tea, that'll fix it.'

Nerida steered her mother into the house and sat her down at the kitchen table. Despite the overcast skies, the kitchen was incandescently bright, causing Mrs Simmonds to cover her face with her hands. Nerida plugged in the jug, embarrassed and capable. It was just an accident. Actually, more of an incident. She's all right. She won't ask me why I did it. Ask me! I'm going off my head with loneliness. Later, Nerida would be ashamed at this display of petulance. And her lover would say, you were just a child. And she would say, but that was no excuse.

'Is my copy ready?' Mrs Simmonds was angry.

'Your copy?'

'My copy! My coffee.'

Coffee was scarcely mentioned in this district. Local Dalmatians were known to drink it from doll-sized cups, but this was a tea-drinking household. Coffee was foreign, which was to say, badly sophisticated.

'I made tea.'

'I'll drink it in my room. I need a lie-down.'

Nerida settled her mother into bed, without undressing her, then returned with the tea. As Mrs Simmonds sipped at the cup she said, 'Don't worry. I'm all right. There are chops for your father. Tell him I've got a headache. There's the spare room.'

'I should call the doctor – '

'No! Go away!'

A small flame of panic licked at Nerida's heart. Her mother never shouted.

23

Her father was tired when he came in and the meat finished him off. He went to sleep in the spare room, designed for another child or for overnight guests, none of whom had eventuated. Nerida wanted to tell him exactly what had happened but talk is hard, especially when a stupidity must be revealed. When he was snoring away she checked on her mother, who was also sleeping peacefully. Nerida sat on the end of the bed and watched her. Mrs Simmonds's breasts were flattened under the blouse. I once must have put my baby mouth over that nipple. I'm so full of craving someone should tie me down. Nerida took after her mother. She saw her own face, its pale skin, the insistent bones, the broad forehead defined by heavy, dark eyebrows in surprising contrast to the blonde hair, reflected on the pillow before her. Except that her mother's face, marked by shadows, was losing its definition. Possibly she had once been beautiful. Mrs Simmonds opened her eyes.

'I've always wanted to go to Mexico.'

'Have you, Mum? I didn't know that.' Neither of Nerida's parents had ever left the country. They had always been rooted to the spot.

Mrs Simmonds frowned, as if struggling with a difficult thought. 'They say, turn the tortilla a second time when the edges just begin to shrivel up. I read that in a library book.'

'Mum –' Nerida wanted to explain herself, but there was no precedent.

'A quick way to make money is to plant beans in October.' Mrs Simmonds began to cry, mucus dribbling from her nose. 'You live two lives. One's happening and the other is the one you are hoping will happen.'

Removing the handkerchief from her sleeve, Nerida wiped her mother's face and wished this tenderness was not confined to a semi-emergency.

'Sorry,' said Mrs Simmonds. 'I've been fine . . . bit drunk.

24

Talking double Dutch, stalking double. Oh well, go to sleep now. I can't thing of a thing.' Curling up underneath the bedspread, she rested her head on her hand with a sigh. Nerida patted her hair and tried to say something sweet but family vocabulary was sparse in that area: there was only the placebo of 'love'; the bathos of 'dear'. She stayed with her until, around two in the morning, reassured by the even rise and fall of her mother's chest, she went to her room, carrying with her the bedside clock so that its ticking would not interfere with Mrs Simmonds's sleep. Nerida fell down on the bed, and kept her foreboding at bay with the promise to return to her mother at dawn.

'Christine!'
You fall asleep. Then you wake up.
'Christine!'
Her father was calling her mother's name like a child wailing for its parent. If Nerida left her bed she would have to face horror and guilt, so she lay there with a pillow over her face. Horror and guilt visited her there anyway, followed by a grief which sank its claws into her, bearing down on her with its hard, black body.

But when she heard the wail of the siren, Nerida dressed quickly and padded to the door of her parents' bedroom. Mr Simmonds was bending over his wife, thumping ineffectually at her chest, breathing into her mouth. Nerida looked away. Her self-disgust was so great she thought she would vomit if she moved. Two men dressed in black uniforms came hurrying along the hallway and pushed past Nerida with their equipment.

Nerida's father kept raking his hair back from his face, which was thin and craggy from lack of sleep, as Nerida described, in a whisper, her mother's fall and subsequent condition. Her voice was reedy, her tone implausible as she excused her failure to summon a doctor with a ludicrous, 'I thought she was all right.' Her mother had died of a subdural haemorrhage. Nerida cried until she was sick and empty and then still hadn't cried enough.

'What kind of stupid fool are you? What kind of stupid – what kind of stupid –?' her father yelled, his voice splintering. He began to weep, a scary, jagged sound, shocking Nerida with the vastness of his emotion. She had had no idea that he loved her mother like that, like an insane lover. He had never said or done anything to indicate it, and he never recovered. The house was deserted, the farm, the family, abandoned.

4

When Drusilla arrived home at mid-term break, Alexis hardly recognised her. She was sixteen but she might as well have been twenty-six, so adult did she look in comparison to spindly Alexis. Drusilla's mouth was thick with lipstick the colour of cherry jam, while her body was encased in a morbid dress cut to defy circulation. Mrs Serafin beamed vaguely at her daughter. She lit another cigarette, forgetting the one already burning in one of five ashtrays prominent in the kitchen, and said, 'Lovely, darling, how decent of them to release you from the uniform.'

'They didn't release me,' Drusilla replied, 'I released myself.'

Mrs Serafin did not respond because she was pouring a glass of wine. Drusilla motioned for Alexis to follow her on to the veranda, leaving their mother alone.

'Did you get into trouble?' Alexis asked, admiring Drusilla's blunt platform boots. 'You could probably knock someone out with those.'

Drusilla jerked her head in the direction of the kitchen. 'Does she still make you rattle on in all those languages?'

'Not so much any more. I think she's forgetting them. I'm glad you're home.'

Drusilla lunged forward and tickled his ribs. Alexis convulsed. 'I only come home to see you, shrimp. Let's face it, Mama and Papa are ultra-strange. You can't rely on them.'

Alexis laughed without saying anything, feeling trapped between loyalty to his parents and love of Drusilla. In her quick way, she saw that he was not throwing all his eggs into her basket. She switched off her affection at the same time as she asked, 'Are you all right? Do you still have those twitches?'

Alexis shrugged goofily. He did not want his parents to know about his occasional lapses.

'I think they should do something about it,' Drusilla added.

'It's nothing,' Alexis whispered.

But she must have told their parents, because a month later Alexis found himself walking the corridor towards his father's study, where two doctors were waiting to test him. One voice in Alexis's head told him that he was fortunate to have so much concern expended on his well-being; a second voice intervened with the suggestion that Drusilla had scored a point, causing his mother and father to feel guilty and useless. It was at this moment in his life that Alexis, unable to commit himself to either faction without inciting a riot of rejection, camped out on the high ground where nothing would bother him. There were things beyond his understanding, but even at this young age, he saw he could use the light armaments of civility and charm to keep confusion at bay. He wouldn't care less about impressing anyone.

'Ah, there he is. Come here, Alexis. Would you like him in this chair, Bateson?'

Alexis's father stood with his hand resting on the creaky leather chair in his study. The doctor, bent over his black bag, straightened and smiled at his patient. Large Dr Bateson stood six feet tall. His features were forceful. There were great curved eyebrows and a strong curve of carved mouth and a massive head of creamed iron-grey hair. He was a grizzly bear to the mink that was Alexis's father.

Dr Serafin was a streak of slender whiteness. Fine-boned, fine ivory hair in shapely cut, fine tailored clothes; the too-natty con-con-continental, they said at Alexis's school. But the missiles of xenophobia launched regularly too by academics and bourgeois neighbours collapsed bluntly against Dr Serafin's actual presence. Once in his drawing room, Dr Serafin's guests, no matter how curmudgeonly their private opinions, were treated with an intimacy that temporarily disarmed them. Used to bondaged English small-talk, fighting their way through boarding-school metaphor and generalised subjectless sentences, the Serafins' guests, medicated by unaccustomed wine, responded like lonely puppies to the you-you-you of Serafin conversation. But this was not the drawing room. This was the exalted study.

'Dr Bugle, my assistant,' said Dr Bateson, inclining his head slightly, and making a littering gesture to indicate a pointy-nosed, barely-adult creature, already tragically bald, standing in a corner. Dr Bugle, notebook in hand, cleared his throat when Alexis met his eyes then turned away and smiled out of the french windows at the winter trees.

I'm not the weakest person in the room, the boy thought.

Dr Bateson stood with one hand on his baron-of-beef hip, the other plunged in his yawning bag. 'Well, I'd rather like him sitting on the desk. Rather easier to –' He made a winding motion in the air. Alexis was not a nervous boy but he was relieved when Dr Bateson pulled from his bag only a harmless stopwatch and a narrow strip of paper about a foot long. He placed these objects on the edge of the desk.

'Very well,' Dr Serafin replied.

But Alexis saw by the way he folded one arm across his chest and, making a precise pincer of his free hand, adjusted his spectacles, that his father was not absolutely happy with the use of the desk, which imposed on the room like an altar. Svelte Dr Serafin had furnished his personal rooms with looming pieces, Biedermeier mostly, as if to affirm that mere size could not dominate him. Alexis settled on the blotter, his legs dangling in the space between two columns of drawers, probably locked. Although he felt there was something sacrilegious about perching on the spot where his father's authoritative pen was producing its immense comparison of Modern English and Modern Czech, the boy was pleased to be the centre of attention.

'Now don't be alarmed. Nothing to it,' said Dr Bateson, taking up the strip of paper between thumb and forefinger.

'I'm not alarmed. Mama explained. A routine hyperventilation test, she said. I'll be interested to see what happens.'

Dr Bateson frowned slightly. Then scooping up the stopwatch, he set the timer with a decisive click. 'Bugle. Notebook now, I think.'

Dr Bugle fluttered into a chair next to the desk. Dr Serafin switched on the anglepoise. Catching his eye, Alexis was rewarded with a nod of encouragement, although his father retreated, his hands clasped behind his back. Standing directly in front of Alexis, Dr Bateson held the strip of paper about twelve inches away from the boy's mouth.

'I want you to blow on this one hundred times. Understand? I shall count the exhalations.' He activated his stopwatch. 'Begin.'

Alexis began to blow. One. The paper quivered. Two. Three. Four. Five . . . After twenty seconds the boy turned his head suddenly to the left while inhaling. A shadow was dancing on the cusp of his vision. His breathing began to labour. He believed he was inflating a huge balloon in his abdomen, a big rubbery sphere, dying to burst out of him. Thirty seconds had elapsed. Just as Alexis was drawing breath for his fifty-second puff, he groaned and clutched at his stomach.

'Facial blanching,' said Dr Bateson.

Alexis felt the balloon deflate violently, spiralling crazily up his throat.

'Followed by blushing.'

Now a raggy thing dropping from his mouth, all its air expelled, delivered him from breathing.

'Tachycardia. Onset abrupt.'

Freed from the gaseous bubble that had been elevating him, Alexis somersaulted head over heels, plunging downwards. He was tumbling towards himself. A vaporous apparition, a genie, rose out of a dark place to meet him, holding in its hands two hemispheres. Alexis's mouth opened and closed, trying to form a scream, but the velocity of his fall tore the sound away.

'Transient hypertension, paroxysmal. Primitive gasping.'

Then he fell right into the genie and, drawn by a powerful draught, plumbed the soft suffocating earth. Now he *was* the genie.

'Alteration in gastric motility. Retching.'

His mouth was full of earth, but he had possessed the hemispheres. His wraith self felt fingers on its carotid artery.

'Pulse a hundred and twenty.'

Having penetrated the earth, he came to rest in a vaulted cave where a banquet had been laid. Fissures in the rock let in sweet, clarifying oxygen. He sucked at it. He was ecstatic. His enriched brain began to feed.

The boy on the desk now threw back his head, drawing a great inspiration. His shudders subsided as he began to breathe more normally. Rocking back and forth, staring at the ceiling, he wrapped his arms around his torso to protect himself from the brilliant cold. An unintelligible stream of words poured from his mouth.

'Alexis!' Springing to the desk, Dr Serafin took his son in his arms. Alexis's head drooped forward until his gaze was

31

once more fixed on the strip of paper which Dr Bateson continued to dangle before him. The doctor depressed his stopwatch.

'Twenty-five seconds have elapsed since the blanching. How many puffs have you managed, Alexis?'

'Fifty-two.'

'Very good. And what happened to you just now?'

Gripping the edge of the desk, Alexis peered between his legs at the murky space between the sets of drawers. He felt pleasantly, beatifically battered, as if something soft but relentless had been pummelling his body, had turned him inside out, had consumed him and licking the bones bare, had placed them delicately on a porcelain plate. He wanted to slide his hand inside his trousers where it was sticky and hot. He wanted to fall into a dreamy sleep. Then he looked at Dr Bateson and his father, one cheerful, the other aghast.

'A genie came out of a cave.'

'That seizure happened when I was thirteen. I'd had meningitis when I was seven and apparently I'd become moody or something so my parents had this experiment done to see if epilepsy was waiting in the wings. From the previous insult to the brain.'

'What happened then?'

'There was a bit of anxious hovering for a while, especially from my mother, but I never had another attack.'

'I've never been ill in my life.' Jane Hinchcliff checked her glowing face in the rear-view mirror and tied back her smooth hair. Alexis kissed her neck. Ignoring the kiss, she buttoned her cardigan. 'I'm meeting my mother at the Imperial. Do I look chaste?'

'As always.'

Jane started up the car, then reversed forcefully out of the narrow lane. They rode along in the blasé silence she favoured after heated interludes in the back seat. She liked tacitly to remind him that their affair was on her terms. 'I don't mean to be promiscuous,' she had said, 'but the odds are that I'll stumble into marriage one day and I hate to think of taking on anything significant without researching it first.'

Alexis appreciated the contrast between Jane's punishing logical-positivist mind and her luscious accommodating body. She was careless with him, often arriving late for rendezvous, rebuking his lack of interest in politics, leaving suddenly after they had made love in the middle of the day, in order to attend a mathematics lecture. He almost loved her. Although Dr and Mrs Serafin were away in Asturias, Jane would never come to Alexis's flat in the Dover Square house his parents had rented for the duration of Dr Serafin's sabbatical. Jane gave Alexis to understand that she was avoiding the sickly closeness of what she referred to, with an astringent turn of the mouth, as Alexis's love-nest; as if he serviced a succession of palpitating girl-undergraduates on pink satin sheets. She reminded him frequently that she was exceptional. A non-dewy nonpareil who had transcended the romantic fantasies contaminating the majority of women.

'My grandmother,' she had said, 'was a suffragette,' causing an image of Jane chained to railings in cotton underwear to sneak into Alexis's mind. He liked her desire to dominate him since without her restraint he might indulge a desire to be adored – and that was tantamount to self-emasculation. At a stroke.

In any case it would not have been easy for her to visit Alexis discreetly, since Moorgate, who shared the flat, was often blundering about. He was afraid of Jane. Moorgate, a good-natured intellectual mediocrity, was ideal to live with. Alexis was free to work or stray into a sedative reverie, without the fever of someone else's cerebration infecting the air.

Jane dropped him in Gower Street, after making an arrangement to see a film with him the following Tuesday. Alexis scrutinised her speeding vintage Prefect until it was out of sight, then turned in the direction of the British Museum. He had an essay to complete but felt too vital, too bacchanalian to work. Besides he preferred to attend to his books at night, after play. After clubs and restaurants, after ballrooms and bedrooms. He believed that scholarship, no matter how crucial the labour at one's desk, doors closed, curtains drawn, was best carried off with a certain discretion, an insouciance, which although in itself was a form of vanity, was nevertheless elegant and sporting, permitting the scholar to move in disguise through the world of men. At University College he was reading English and Anthropology. He sauntered through these studies while reserving the real force of his intellect for a private pursuit of the works of the American anthropologist and linguist, Samuel Zeugen, famous for his study of Plains Indians.

Occasionally, when he was a child, Drusilla had taken him to the cinema instead of the library. His preference had been for cowboy and Indian films. The cowboys, with their limited repertoire of manly endeavours and the dead hand of righteousness lying on them, failed to move him, but the Indian tribes possessed beautiful names. Sioux. Crow. Cheyenne. Dakota. Cree. Apache. When they rode out to battle, the young warriors used a secret warpath language. They lived a dangerous life of dancing, blood and decoration. And in the night-time (although here he'd had to use his imagination), they crawled under animal skins with lovely women whose black hair hung in long sinuous braids. Words attached to the Indian world were full of mysterious potential. Medicine Arrows. Medicine Lodge. Medicine Lake. They made him want to crack them open.

This interest led Alexis to Samuel Zeugen whose name

jumped at him one day from his father's bookshelves. Dr Serafin, suffering in later years from intellectual disdain, had come to dismiss Zeugen's work. He was not engaged by Zeugen's general investigation of the flight of the individual into artistic endeavour.

'Psychology,' he would say, flicking his wrist. 'Look at his attitude to the phoneme.' Dr Serafin held to the structural view of phonemes as signs of differentiation. The practical rugger-playing British, on the other hand, perceived the phoneme as a physical entity. But Zeugen was more abstract. He considered a family of speech sounds – family: Papa, Mama, Drusilla, me – to be variants of one ideal sound.

'Papa, don't you think the aim of the ideal is embedded in language?'

'The ideal?' Dr Serafin clapped his hand to his temple as if stung by an insect. For some minutes his eyes remained closed, either ruminating on the foolishness of his son, or casting his mind back to a time when his own opinions had been invigorating and unified.

Alexis was at a loss to explain why this misty-eyed linguistic view should appeal so strongly to him, a boy brought up in a structuralist frame of mind. No bare-chested braves galloped through the cobbled streets of Prague or the silent asphalted streets of Auckland. But Zeugen suggested to Alexis the necessity of long journeys through recalcitrant terrain, marked by the occasional weathered sign, a desiccated body lying near by, which said: 'THIS WAY TO HEAVENLY DESTINATION'. A destination so utter, you had no language to describe it.

Moreover, Alexis needed the focus of Samuel Zeugen, as an exemplar. Zeugen had been a traveller and a man of romantic disposition, yet he had harnessed this dreamy nature to the rigours of intellectual enquiry. Alexis kept Samuel Zeugen fixed in his head in order to prevent himself from capitulating to something weak and feckless in his character which existed because he was too naturally clever. Everything came easily. He had been brought up to achieve greatness, but deep in his heart there lurked a kind of boredom. A laziness. He felt his mind to be both full and vacant.

In the museum Alexis lingered, thinking of Jane, in front of the Greek kraters used by symposia hosts for mixing wine. Black figures on red. Red figures on black. He was twenty-one.

5

A roll of thunder woke Nerida. She could not make out a thing in the unfamiliar room at first. Reacting to the approach of a storm, she drew the covers up around her ears and wriggled cosily as rain pattered overhead, or in the walls of wherever she was. Reaching for her watch, she saw that it was 6.15 a.m. Ten minutes later, another barrage of thunder shook the house, followed by a gurgling that now sounded less like rain. Slowly it dawned on her that she was listening to the rumble of underground trains passing through nearby Edgware Tube Station interspersed with the hiccoughing of the building's heating system. She was no longer in a place where the elements were primary. She was in London. With a sigh of relief, Nerida rolled on to her stomach and returned to sleep.

When Nerida descended on London at the fag-end of a northern winter, she spent her first week in a bed and breakfast, where she used up the first twenty minutes of her future consulting the work section of a visitors' guide. Agency nursing was mentioned, along with secretarial work, English-language teaching, and council services, 'for instance, positions as play-group leaders or assistants in homes for the elderly'. Other less skilled alternatives proposed were bar work, dispatch riding, catering, 'or possibly, work in a betting shop'.

Hours after Nerida's arrival, an unusually helpful woman

at a bureau de change, while diminishing Nerida's dollars in the conversion to sterling, had explained that Australian and New Zealand girls were much in demand as nannies and housekeepers. They were known to be reliable and practical. They could drive cars and steam vegetables. Unruly animals did not bother them. They could be counted on to console wailing infants and highly strung mothers. They were unlikely to have sex with their employers. Nerida closed the guide. She was not destined for any of these things.

Instead, she ran down four flights of stairs and threw herself into the city. At first sight, London was dirty and daunting, but Nerida instinctively appreciated its talent for eccentricity; for anonymity. Boys selling umbrellas and alarm clocks on Oxford Street called her 'darling' and she thought: This place is fantastic. As large as history and as small as a sandwich bar. She understood at once that London, although forbidding, despised seriousness, relishing the skill it took to be deeply trivial. The streets were alive with decadent shoes and demanding pop music and revolutionary hairstyles, which diverted attention from internal confusions of mind. A newcomer, unconfident of her grasp of art and culture, would be delighted to find that London couldn't care less.

English newspapers were full of outrage at the failure of spring. Pallid pedestrians regarded the low skies with resentment. But Nerida was exhilarated by the sudden blast of cold air. Her many varieties of fear, for so long nourished in isolation like exotic plants in a glasshouse, shrivelled up one by one as they became exposed to a change of climate. Snow fell on her past and covered it over.

Alighting from a taxi outside Selfridge's, Nicholas Preston, the photographer, noticed a striking girl darting through the traffic towards him. She moved well, like someone used to exercise. Her hair was blonde and she wore a white Mexican wedding shirt over loose white trousers, a costume completely wrong for the season. As he assessed her – she had paused in front of one of Selfridge's windows – a cutaneous tingling overtook him. This was not primarily a sexual response. The excitement lay in discovering a new conduit for his ideas in the form of her novel face. He watched the girl at a little distance, seeing that she examined with discernment the passersby and her surroundings. Her gaze consumed handbags, beards, litter, doorhandles, the small print on shop signs, the pattern of road-markings, the number of buttons on assorted overcoats. She transmitted a strong signal which he could not ignore. Nicholas's intuition, where it served the advancement of his career, was unerring.

When he finally convinced Nerida to visit his studio, she remarked that in the late thirties and early forties some physicists had used photographic emulsions to detect cosmic rays. He thought this was charming. During the test-sitting she reminded him that Pierre Curie was tragically killed in a road accident in 1906, which made Nicholas laugh. He liked a whimsical girl. Nerida was bubbly and clear like a glass of soda water, but when she was photographed, as Nicholas saw with satisfaction as he examined the contact sheets, she became darker and richer, more intoxicating. He took her on a shoot to Spain.

While the heat of Cádiz seized them, Nicholas ran around her in his photo-journalist way, crying, 'Talk to me as if you were angry. Go on. Speak now!'

Nerida strode through the locations. She said, 'Well, the world is underpinned by concealed symmetries. What else makes me desolate? Any consideration of violent progression. I'm familiar with your camera. Sprocket wheels have teeth that engage the film's perforations. The term "gate" refers to the pressure plate. How much information can one person absorb before she becomes actively volcanic? I envy fat middle-class people with their houses and gardens and their regularity. For me, the harvest is bad and I'd like to learn the dance steps that lead to possession.'

'Good girl. Good *National Geographic* girl. Keep on. I want your mouth moving.'

'I'm pissed off, Nicky. A house is burning down! A garden is dying!'

Nerida fell silent while Nicholas changed cameras. And then she said, 'Why am I saying such ridiculous things? I don't feel intelligent.'

A woman ran to Nerida and dusted her cheeks with blusher and sprayed her hair with distilled water and then retired suddenly as Nicholas, delicately adjusting the new lens, ran at his subject. 'Intelligence is not the issue. It's the effect of intelligence. You can do that. Clever baby. Sad girl. That's a good look. Tell me what's happening.'

'Uh. I don't know.'

'I don't care about logic. No one's listening.'

'I'm walking through the desert with the Zar-sickness. I need help but the curer, the Zar-father, is being interviewed by French ethnographers who will later become famous for being French ethnographers . . .' Nerida kicked off her sandals and walked barefoot in the sand. It wasn't painful at all, not like the black West Coast sands of New Zealand that glittered brilliantly in the sun and seared the soles off your feet so that you were always running for shade.

The resulting photographs, published in the name of fashion, made Nerida desirable and dilated Nicholas's reputation.

He photographed her in evening clothes treading desolately the streets of the East End. As soon as he activated the camera she began speaking, conversing not with Nicholas, but with the lens. 'On the subject of love,' she said, 'a painful practice is required. It is necessary to be disgusted, disappointed, humiliated, hysterical, euphoric, insanely altered. This may add up to nothing. There is nothing you can do, but do whatever presents itself. Often it will not be enough. Do not allow yourself to be eaten by the head of an old philologist. Do not allow anyone to accuse you in the *zócalo*.'

On the subject of love, Nerida was uncommitted, casual and amusing. She liked a joke. On the subject of love, she told Nicholas when he made his inevitable move, she was not interested. And nor, truthfully, was he. He was enthralled only by his photographs because in executing them he was masterful. Nerida and Nicholas, having recognised one another as fellow fantasists, did not have to bother with an actual romantic relationship, which would have been destructive to their professional intercourse.

Since everyone was so pleased with her, Nerida was pleased with herself. The make-up sessions, the expensive clothes, the cameras, these were of consequence. They lavished care on her, more so than any man could do. In the process, Nerida smartened up. She became an expert at self-scrutiny in her bathroom. For three years she worked incessantly, impersonating an adored woman, and at any time she could pour through her model's book and confirm that she existed, until an unwelcome melancholy intruded upon her effervescent life. It coincided with a change in Nicholas's perception of his work.

During the time Nerida had known him, he had slowly turned away from his early *en passant* street style in favour of detailed, complicated narrative sequences which were time-consuming to arrange. The spontaneity he sought – the leap from a bus, the champagne glass flung in anger – could no longer be trusted to spring to his satisfaction from the authentic world. This spontaneity took for ever. And the crazy things that Nerida had said on the spur of the moment during their sessions, Nerida staring earnestly into the camera telling nobody in particular that American soldiers fighting at Dunkirk had subsisted on battle rations of one or two chocolate bars a day, whose three thousand calories fuelled them with enough energy to fight without fainting, now Nicholas demanded them of her. He wanted her to write them down. They would collaborate on a series of surreal narratives. But when he said that, all her inspiration evaporated, and he began to use her less.

While Nicholas and his many intimidated assistants laboured at the consummate set-up, Nerida watched and waited, growing bored. She played with her bracelets while crisis hung around the studio like somebody's tough working-class boyfriend, small-minded and ambiguously glamorous. A strategic bouquet of flowering thyme wilted under the lights. A chair became too small or too tall for the frame. A woman became too small or too tall for the frame, causing temper tantrums that bordered on mental illness. Having moved among artistic types in the last three years, Nerida had become practised at choosing a position in the calm eye of the storm, even one that raged in a teacup. She was adept at avoiding involvement.

As she found less to amuse her in the studios and on the streets she felt forced to take up an activity to fill the endless hours. Since photography was all she knew, she bought a camera and equipped a darkroom. The subjects of her photographs were of no concern. She was indiscriminate, aiming her camera everywhere. The importance of photography lay in its mechanical and chemical functions which completely claimed her attention, preventing her from squandering time or succumbing to the melancholy.

She appreciated the darkroom which contrasted extremely with her viciously illuminated bathroom. Nicholas Preston's picking her up had been a stroke of luck, but contrary to superficial judgements about models, she was not vain enough to believe that the work would continue without maintenance of her face and body. Every morning she stood between two full-length mirrors, subjecting herself to the remorseless honesty of fluorescent lighting, and in these exacting conditions she practised transformations. The torso twisted into *contrapposto* tightened and reduced her waist. The head held at a certain angle exoticised her features, while an up-from-under look infantilised them, making her variable and marketable. She manipulated herself. Through her body she made a study of illusion.

And as she found less to amuse her in the studios and on the streets, and in between taking photographs and applying lipstick, Nerida sometimes caught a glimpse of a parallel universe. Someone had once said to her, you live two lives.

You climb out of bed, shrugging off sleep, dodging death, and step on to the balcony. The air is sharp. The sound of sparse, early morning traffic is reassuring. Human beings are abroad. Men and women contracted to projects and aims. Thinking about their children and SpaceWorld 4000 and tennis stars and Gödel's Second Incompleteness Theory. Men and women in love. Fetishists and members of gyms. Women with fancy handwriting and men with a desire to write letters. Women enchanted by the elegance of geometrical forms and men plagued by conscience. Women plagued by ambiguity and men enchanted by the groves of academe or the fall of pleated skirts.

You feel kind of amphetamined, although nothing is polluting your blood. Have you settled in? Well, get ready to settle out! How far have we really come? You say again, how far have I really come? You believe you're wearing silver boots with wings on the ankles and your brain's been boosted and the swimming pool looks great at night lit by underwater lights and a hit-me-right-here song is playing. You know all the words. You could zoom into space and free-radical your way into a highly symmetrical psychic situation where the weak and electromagnetic forces are the same.

You are massive and delighted by life.

You choose to drink a Riviera – rum, cointreau, framboise – and eat a rocket salad.

You're as warm as a sable muff and just as symbolic.

You're impervious enough to stop bullets.

Your kissing's so good it causes stellar evolution.

Nerida was, in essence, an optimist.

6

Four days after he had last seen Jane, Alexis woke with his mind in a tempest. He splashed icy water on his face. He shook his head from side to side to escape the heavy net that had fallen on him, but the net stayed. Ignoring Moorgate's cheerful greeting, Alexis left the house without saying goodbye. Outside he encountered pleasant weather. The wind had dropped. Flowers bloomed in the square. But Moorgate, watching from the sitting-room window, saw Alexis stiffen and set his face, apparently.making his way in the teeth of a howling nor'wester. Alexis was not accustomed to being tossed about by moods. As the day wore on he could find no reason for his fury at breaking a nib, or for his contemptuous rage when a man in his year argued sophistically, or for his despair at the uselessness of the university itself.

On his return he remembered that he was supposed to take Jane to the cinema. Jane, who could not be bothered with post-coital endearments. As she entered his mind, rising from the rumpled sheets to fly to her all-embracing lemmata, the net tightened around him, constricting his perception of her to one sulky thought: she was a cold bitch who would not love him. He left a short telephone message for her, cancelling their arrangement, then sank into bed thinking of Drusilla. He would like to talk to her but she was in Greece capturing the secrets of something. Throughout his adolescence, Drusilla had talked to him of blood and kinship and he had become anthropological. That was her influence, as much as his father's, and he was grateful for it. But then she'd flown away and taken all her intimate talk with her. If you insist that the world is complicated you could at least offer an explanation or some dumb comfort, Alexis fumed, forgetting that he'd made a pact with himself to be carefree, instead of flitting here and there leaving me with the homesickness.

Wednesday was even blacker. After an insomniac night, he'd finally fallen asleep at dawn so that when he arose groggily it was already mid-morning and the day's schedule was in disarray. Moorgate, embarrassed by Alexis's bad form, had left a note. 'Not back till last possible moment. M.' Well, fuck him. Alexis stayed indoors, too lethargic to dress or eat, while bulky thoughts bumped around his brain like sinister Zeppelins darkening the sky. Reading failed him, even Zeugen's first, usually luminous, collection of poems, *NarZiss*. Alexis was possessed by an anguish so keen, it immobilised him.

Late in the afternoon or early evening, as he sat by the dead fire, a fresh, salty tang of the sea flooded into the room, swirled about for a moment, and then receded. Since Alexis was staring at the aqua walls of the sitting room, he thought he had made a glancing marine connection between colour and smell. He felt afraid. Then he became overwhelmingly aware of the book lying on the tea-table beside his armchair. Zeugen – which led, like a flame racing along a fuse, to: *NarZiss*. Zed. Zayin. A weapon. Zeus. Lightning bolts, attributes of. Z. Sometimes disguised as a double S. Stormtrooper. Night of the Long Knives. Zayin. A weapon. Alien letter of the Roman alphabet. Terminal letter. Death letter. Suicide note. Pull the trigger. Zeugen found floating in green water. ZZZ. Sleep.

Alexis's fingers began to drum softly on the table top while his gaze was drawn up and slightly to his left.

A photic Z appeared on the wall, shimmering. Pulsating. Projected from an incandescent source behind his eyes. A physiological vibration coincided with the visual flicker, as at the back of his throat his glottis opened and closed voicing the letter Z. Suddenly, his body jerked as the zigzag of light thrust at him. It lanced through his eyes, igniting a fierce cranial storm. It struck at the architecture of his brain. Structures reeled, collapsed and were swallowed up by fissures in the earth.

He managed to reach his bed. A metallic taste was in his mouth. Tenderly he lay down, dragging the sheet to his chin. Every movement intensified the pain in his head, which was full of sharp things, sabre, scissors, razor, dentist's drill, preventing him from sleeping. But as time passed he drifted in and out of consciousness. Despite the agony of moving, he had sometimes to get up over the following twenty-four hours for water, or he would have dehydrated. He pissed copiously, sweated buckets, vomited bile. At one point someone, a doctor smelling of boiled cabbage, had his fingers at Alexis's wrist. By Thursday afternoon, the worst was over. The headache ebbed away, leaving him stranded on his bed, light-headed and enervated.

Alexis took a glass of water from a person who bore an amazing resemblance to Moorgate. He could not remember if the two of them had finished a conversation or if a question or an incomplete thought was still hovering in the air. There was something Moorgate needed to know. Alexis gulped at the water, then closed his hand on Moorgate's wrist.

'Listen. My father, Antonin Serafin, was born in Prague.'

Moorgate wore an alarmed grin, but nodded encouragingly.

'He studied at the Caroline University where he was

severely influenced by the work of the comparativist Josef Zubaty.' Horrible tears sprang into Alexis's eyes. 'Papa, he's a man who has been fucked by geography! When he was only twenty-five he delivered an outstanding lecture at one of the sittings of the Royal Czech Learned Society. You wouldn't have heard of it, certainly not you of all people. The lecture, extrapolated from his doctoral thesis, was a very clever, plausible argument for a synchronistic analysis of language. He was ahead of his time.'

'I dare say he was!' Moorgate broke in, a big stupid smile on his big stupid face. Alexis wanted to punch him. For being an idiot. Because the interior of Moorgate's mind was not a black pit. Moorgate shrank a little from Alexis's smouldering stare.

'He thought linguists should examine the state of a system as it functions at a particular time rather than looking back through time. He attacked the complacency of linguistic studies. He looked away from the problems of historical grammar. Are you paying attention? I said he looked away from the problems of historical grammar. But the significance of Papa's avant-garde synchronism was not appreciated. Prague at that time wasn't intellectually regarded. You can imagine what happened.'

Moorgate wrinkled his brow, slightly desperate. He would be pulling on what he referred to as his thinking cap, which never seemed to fit. Olympian Alexis watched Moorgate struggle.

'Nobody came to the lecture?'

'Of course people came to the lecture! This was Prague, not bloody Shropshire or something. People don't knit in Prague. They have ideas.'

Moorgate tugged at a knot on his chest, embarrassed. He was wearing an endless fawn pullover whose pattern of cables petered out in a confusion of sagging stitches and knots. This was the handiwork of Moorgate's aristocratic rural mother, who liked to indulge in a craft from time to time. Alexis ignored Moorgate's discomfort.

'He delivered the paper in the wrong language. It was in Czech, which is not a world language. He should have read his paper in Moscow. Or in Geneva. He would have made an impact if it had been in French or Russian. Papa's second geographical mistake was to leave Prague and follow my mother to London. I know. It's heartbreaking. He should have become part of the Prague Linguistic Circle but instead he was screwing my mother in London where nothing was happening linguistically. When he decided they should return to Prague, the Nazis got there before him and closed down the universities. Have you actually ever had a woman, M? I can't imagine you have.'

A painful blush crossed his friend's face. Alexis wanted to weep again. He was behaving like a monster. He wasn't himself. He had no idea why he was tormenting Moorgate like this, and enjoying the sensation of violence.

'Well, Mama, she's short and dark, or used to be. Voluptuous. She had a lot of wiry, wavy hair. Drusilla said she said it was a relief when fashion let her cut it. Lifted a weight off her shoulders. Mama inherited the money from her grandfather. Sheffield steel. She roamed around Europe doing the silly courses that girls do, cordon bleu and sketching in the Tyrol. But she was actually intelligent. Particularly good at languages. Before I went away to school she amused herself, and me, by using a different language for each day of the week. We spoke English at weekends, which was when they held their parties and she was at her most animated. English to me is a language of anticipation, of suppressed excitement, of crystal and silver and velvet and excellent food. Her name is Caroline, did I mention that?

'She met him in Prague. She went to one of his lectures

and said she admired his methodological discipline. Ha! I suppose he bought her coffee and cakes afterwards. Probably kissed her a bit, that sort of thing. Anyway, he got stuck on English. He wrote an essay for her, 'On the Phonological System of Modern English', but still with the same preoccupation. You know, language as a complex of mutually interdependent facts. It's mouldering in his study somewhere, or perhaps it was left behind in Prague. He also left behind what had been a most productive collaboration with Sergej Karcevskij. Once he abandoned the university he never held a worthwhile academic post again.

'My parents emigrated. I've only lately realised that they were simply on holiday. Karcevskij became a professor at Geneva University. Karcevskij. Doesn't that name – doesn't that name seem really inspiring?'

Moorgate, laying a damp cloth across Alexis's forehead, whispered, 'Steady on, Serif.' Sometime later Moorgate reappeared at Alexis's bedside, his square hands flexing in search of a task.

'I'm quite hungry.'

Relieved at the recession of the personal, Moorgate punched one hand into the other. 'Right-oh. Crumpets and a brew-up. By the way, a migraine, Dr Gooch said. Got a prescription for pills and potions.'

'Thank you.'

'Doesn't seem like you, Serif, stretched out on the *chaise-longue*. You gave me a start, you know.'

'Same.'

Once bathed, shaved and dressed, Alexis consumed the crumpets and drained the tea-pot, letting Moorgate ramble on. Moorgate was saying to his teacup, 'And then I ran into Jane Hinchcliff. Very polar on the subject of you, I'm afraid.' Alexis had the impression he'd behaved badly there but was too exhausted to untangle that particular thread of recall. Tackle the awful backlash later.

Returning to bed, he fell into a deep sleep. But he was pulling open the curtains. Dawn had barely arrived. In the night something seismic had occurred. White mist drifted over a flooded crater. The mist, which he realised now was steam, billowed over a wide pool, his fluid, hissing mind, in which was suspended the glittering traces of every idea he'd had, every book he'd read, every emotion experienced. These brilliant deposits – antimonious orange, arsenical green, sulphurous yellow – shifted and rose, making their presence known.

Too agitated to make the fire, Alexis switched on the electric. He ate breakfast while standing. Without bothering to dress, he sat at his desk and filled his pen. His hand began to exercise itself upon the paper. He wrote: 'The vitality of the verb, the value of the interjection, the cunning of the conjunction. The instability. Two poles. Magnetism, all the usual antipodes. Language, its relentless productivity. Crossfire. He was an artist. He was a linguist. Dualism was innate in the man himself. Sergej Karcevskij's "Du dualisme asymétrique du signe linguistique."'

Screwing up the notes, Alexis took a fresh sheet of paper. Although it was more than a year since he had read Karcevskij's brief essay, in a journal belonging to his father, his memory delivered it to him without omission. Karcevskij was absorbed by the slippage between the phonic sign and its meaning. The development of language depended on this tense dualism. Retrograde to explain linguistic change through the vagaries of the human psyche. Papa was right. An ample rich etcetera filled Alexis. He began to write involuntarily at a pitch of apprehension as remarkable for its ease as its acumen.

Eight weeks later the same sequence of insomnia, bad

51

temper and the searing Z manifested itself. Headache, vomiting, deep sleep. In the serene aftermath of the second attack, Alexis wrote another automatic paper, this time on the subject of syntax, comparing forms of predication in English and Czech. English: preferring fixity in its word order and a penchant for the passive voice. Czech: a less congealed word order; the active voice. He flew on to anatomise the contrasting treatment of the grammatical subject, showing how the use of the dative in Modern Czech functioned similarly to its use in Old English. Then swerved into a comparison of nominal English versus verbal Czech. Under the intermittent influence of Z, nothing could staunch Alexis's precocious, teeming production.

7

Those who eventually witnessed Alexis's friendship with Eugene Rinehart were surprised that urbane Alexis would bother with a man who metaphorically sat on a porch-swing chewing a blade of hay, despite his academic achievements. Aside from their professional concerns, nobody could see what they had in common, although it was true that the dramatic circumstances in which they had met might have forged a bond. Eugene had saved Alexis's life, elliptically, in Michigan where they were attending a conference concerning sign languages, a subject Eugene had explored, with particular reference to secretiveness, in his doctoral thesis.

Eugene was a direct, even ingenuous cartoon of a man, but his professional focus on the arcane, on the covert signing of athletes, hunters, scouts, masons and vagabonds, demonstrated, at least to himself, that he was capable of divining mystery. Disappointed from birth by his lack of innate poetic ability, he had managed by means of meticulous research and the faithful recording of others' lives to accomplish a sense of himself as a complex, astonishing person: the sum of all his subjects' parts. As he processed their secrets, he became in his mind's eye tanned and well built, a man of graceful gestures and an enigmatic way with language, a seducer and an instigator. Only his actual appearance let him down. And his inability, once he was cast adrift from his desk, to speak to women without feeling that he was eight years old, a pre-pubescent babbler in shorts and a striped T-shirt. Look at this slingshot I made, it's really neat! You can visit me in my tree hut, if you want to.

Where Eugene toiled, Alexis relaxed. His first submissions to the British graduate periodical, *Lingo*, had been accepted readily by the impressed editors. Only months after he had gained his First, journals in France and America sought Alexis's contributions, and in those countries he was spared the suspicious criticism of him expressed occasionally in England, where brilliance was considered improper if not unnatural. Dispatching his doctorate with ease, he formed tangential, fleeting attachments to various universities and centres of higher study. Fortified by his family's money, Alexis was at liberty to explore ideas without taking on the burden of teaching and administration. He dressed and ate well. He travelled. Life was perilously beneficent, waiting in the shadows with a flick knife up its sleeve, giving him the chance to be a hero or a victim. It might or might not strike, depending on whether Alexis strayed into the bad part of town.

When the date and subject of the Michigan conference was announced, Eugene embarked on a fretful period of writing and rewriting, sweating over the placement of footnotes and the accuracy of his bibliography. He was comforted during this long detention by delusions of grandeur and frequent meals of pizza and potato salad. Alexis, on the other hand, enjoyed several pleasant recesses in Portugal, Madrid and Cîteaux in France where he excavated lists of signs used in Cistercian monasteries. He lingered for a while in the cul-de-sac of the cloisters knowing that the handful of scholars who compiled esoteric dictionaries would be grateful for any tidbit of information flung into the mouth of the caves where they laboured. And having discovered that Claire Smith, a temporary lover, and wife of a colleague in London, would be accompanying her husband to Ann Arbor, Alexis was easily motivated to manufacture a lecture. The conference would enhance his academic standing while allowing him to indulge in Claire. Few women interested Alexis for more than several weeks at a time. He had noticed a pattern, of course. Something cool and restrained in the manner of regimental stripes. Jane Hinchcliff repeated. He chose women who admired him but had other things on their minds or were married, or both.

Then at the conference, Alexis unexpectedly fell into a depression, although it was concealed from all but himself and, possibly, Claire. The vital element of neglect that she had contributed to their intrigue had disappeared on her arrival at Ann Arbor. She had asked questions. She had begun to telephone him constantly. Even now she was occupying an illegal seat in the auditorium, attracting sidelong glances from those who knew her and her husband. Alexis commanded the podium in the conference centre with all his usual élan, it seemed, intact. He began with a witticism which energised his audience and then set sail on the watertight craft of his lecture, slicing through seas which ran smooth and deep, his attentive colleagues already mentally clapping. But he was aware of Claire gazing down on him from her distant seat, with a naked, crabbed expression on her face. She might just as well have been holding a sign that read: 'Reproach'.

Monk, cell, habit, rule. In the Cistercian case, expression of individuality has the capacity to destroy. The previous evening in his hotel room the radiators had been turned up too high and it had been impossible to adjust them. Outside, thick falling snow baffled all sound. Claire's body was like a furnace. She lay full-length on top of him, her tongue slithering into his ears. She lay upside-down beside him and sucked his ankles. She was so full of emotion she seemed radioactive, contaminating him, stiffening his penis

55

but causing the remainder of his being to become weak and ineffective. He did not move. He lay on the bed in the position of a corpse while her head of soft, wavy hair swept up and down his belly. After a few minutes, she sat up, frowning.

'Help me,' she said. 'What do you want?'

'I don't know. I'm preoccupied by my paper.'

'That's unlike you.'

'Cistercian monasteries, where speech is proscribed for much of the time, divide their lexicon into three groups.'

'I see. It's a diversion.'

'So shoot me. I don't know what I want.'

Claire continued to stare at him, disappointed. Since he did not care to examine his desire to excommunicate her, he stroked her hair and told her she was beautiful and if she was angry with him she could do anything she wanted. The muscles in Claire's fresh English face tightened.

'I want to hire somebody to beat you up,' she said, 'and leave you with bruises and a lot of pain. Tell me what you are thinking.'

He was thinking that the primary authorised list of signs reflects the official way of life in the Order, but he said, 'You could hit me. Hurt me. Dig your fingernails into my throat. Piss on me, I don't care.'

But she did not respond to that invitation. Instead she kissed his face affectionately and then lay on her side, stroking his arm, waiting for him to come to his senses, unable to understand why he had resisted the orgasm she had offered him. He did not know why himself. He wished he were in a trance state at that moment in which all decision was taken care of and he was a perfect automaton without responsibility. When he entered the Z-world his emptiness was filled and his indiligence, which he glimpsed in his relationships with women, was banished.

In order to depersonalise the atmosphere and further to

antagonise her, Alexis told Claire that an authorised list, attached to individual abbeys, deviates from the traditional list in its use of dialect forms or particular expressions deriving from whatever manufacture of products takes place. These deviations are tolerated only in the particular monastery that originated them. Then he made her get dressed which she did, at first reluctantly, then with anger. But before she could put her shoes on, he pushed her back on the bed and insinuating his fingers inside, began compulsively to caress her. She was already slippery. She was frowning and sighing.

Not to mention the list of original signs from a named abbey. These are personal, sometimes idiosyncratic additions to the sparse official inventory. This list has the advantage of establishing rapport in a community as well as widening the scope of communication. She threw her arms around his neck. He understood that she wanted him to push his cock inside her but she didn't say anything and neither did he. Removing his hand from between her legs, he fell down beside her, drained, disinterested.

'I think sexuality is about repression,' she said. 'Sometimes when you let it out, there's nothing there. Or there's too much there to cope with.'

His mouth tasted sour. He talked to her for a while without answering her observation, and combed her hair and then she left the room.

As the signs become more personalised, they are not only not recognised in other monasteries, but the favouring of the individual threatens the monastic ideal. Alexis could not fathom why he had become so heartless, so loathsome, suddenly incapable of pleasure. Probably, he told himself, it had to do with the singular operations of his brain. Recently, he could not tell if his thoughts were original or if he was simply replicating what he had read in manuscripts which had not yet been disseminated.

57

When they were, he would be revealed as an ignoble imposter.

The previous year he had spent a summer in the West of Ireland researching a lonely episode of Samuel Zeugen's life. Alexis had not yet published a single word directly on the subject of Zeugen, who was a revelation to be held in reserve. In Sligo, pacing the low-ceilinged room where Zeugen had written a desperate volume dedicated to his dead wife, Alexis envied that creativity and its motivation. There must have been a transformational anguish. Not grammar. In his own heart, passion and resistance were locked in a punitive embrace.

The night before the conclusion of the conference, Eugene was skittering along the icy pavement towards the Linz Austrian Restaurant, thinking of monks and grilled ribs, when he saw Alexis Serafin and Claire Smith emerge blatantly from the Linz. About to pull on a glove, Claire stared in consternation at her hand, then turned abruptly and re-entered the restaurant. As Alexis unlocked the driver's door of his hired Mustang, Eugene waved vigorously, although he and Alexis had only been briefly introduced at an inaugural cocktail party. Unbalanced by his frantic greeting, Eugene lost his footing and collapsed in the dirty snow. At once Alexis left his car. He had hardly helped Eugene to his feet when a careening truck ran a red light, lost control and smashed screechingly into the side of the Mustang. The driver's door was folded back on the steering wheel, its glass shattered, its chrome trim sticking up like a broken bone. Alexis, Eugene and passersby stood about for a minute or two, stunned, then people came running out of the restaurant, including Claire who gazed from the car to Alexis and back to the car again. With great concentration she drew on her gloves. The truck-driver, his face bleeding, staggered from the cab. No death had occurred. The Linz's patrons eventually finished their meals and Alexis finished with Claire, or vice versa.

Raising the frosted glass mid-sentence to his small, pouting mouth, Eugene was struck by another observation. His hand jerked in emphasis, slopping the whisky sour on to the bar where he and Alexis were enduring the countdown before their respective flights to Los Angeles and London. He was delighted to have met Dr Serafin, who was the template of all he desired to be. Eugene wore a creased tie, which he patted repeatedly as his conversation became more torrential. Having discoursed upon the humilation of Little League, on the uncertainty of his student years, the benefits of sleeping in a hammock and the historical significance of Mexican food, Eugene was now launched on the signing of American Plains Indians, a practice that had fallen into decline.

'I like the old things,' said Eugene. 'I like tradition. I like to get back. You know what I mean?' This wasn't very scholarly but he felt he could talk frankly with Alexis, let himself go. There are very few people you can really talk to.

In passing he mentioned the name of Samuel Zeugen, but Alexis did not divulge his own fascination with the man. Eugene failed to notice that, although Alexis was a lively, attentive companion, he delivered very little personal detail. That was one of Alexis's skills, the appearance of familiarity, of amity, of rapprochement. He chose his words with great care without seeming to do so.

Eugene's interest in Indian culture was to take him to the south of Mexico in June. A grateful recipient of a grant from the Smithsonian, his ambition was to write a grammar of Tzotzil, the language of Indians living in and around Zinacantan. People of the Bat. They spoke one of perhaps thirty Mayan languages still in use. Unfortunately large numbers of anthropologists had already infiltrated the area and at least one other academic was at this moment compiling a dictionary of Tzotzil, but Eugene hoped that he could clear a patch for himself among this investigative multitude and begin to cultivate a career. He invited Alexis to visit him at any time, especially in Mexico, and speculated upon the stimulating episodes they might enjoy there. *Hombre a hombre*. And then laughed at himself for the presumption.

Alexis liked that laugh. He was drawn to Eugene as a type. He was just the sort he often befriended, at the very least because a man like Eugene showed a man like Alexis to advantage. Despite the nightmare of his clothes, Eugene was intelligent and possessed, Alexis suspected, a mulishness that would make him a dependable travelling companion in difficult circumstances. Alexis perceived him as a Moorgate with brains. Moorgate himself had been swallowed up by the past, having inherited the family estate and a connected obsession with the breeding of champion rams.

Eugene's flight was imminent. He and Alexis shook hands. Eugene's fingers were gritty with salt from the hundreds of peanuts he had consumed in the foregoing hour. After watching Eugene's rotund frame, made even bulkier by his huge plaid overcoat, disappear through the glass doors of the bar, Alexis hurried to the restroom and flung water on his face. His mood was foul. You arsehole, you piece of shit, he snarled at the wavering face in the mirror. He prayed that his flight would not be delayed. Already a headache had struck. But he felt reassured too, like a woman noticing the fresh flow of menstrual blood, that an essential cycle was manifesting itself.

Alexis had come to regard his epilepsy as a gift from the gods. Spared the twitchings of *grand mal*, his seizures were subjective, hallucinatory, but with a retention of awareness and memory that allowed him to process them. The ZZZs which signalled the onset of his automatism exerted their power only at intervals designated by his temporal lobes. At other times he could look on a Z without effect although he did find his eye increasingly drawn to that letter if only to confirm that its potency was not constant. Gradually a pattern emerged that structured and supplied his intellectual life, allowing him to arrange a work schedule accommodating the onslaught. He came to depend on his condition for the release of a spectacular, decisive self. There had been no reason to consult a physician since he did no damage to himself or others and in any case he would have been reluctant to reveal an affliction. Unmanly to cry out.

8

Nerida was sitting at a black glass table, too small for the numbers squashed around it, watching from time to time the supra-human transvestites on stage at Le Jaguar. She had all the money she needed, all the drinks she could buy, she had enough appetite to eat up an entire buffet. The club was hot, tiny and very dark, reminding Nerida of a cave. Because she was tired, she allowed an uncontrolled image to torment her: she hovered above the table waiting for a guest to come to her house, her bat-cave. He ate her meal, although only after he had had a long struggle to arrive; he had almost expired. When it was midnight, and nearly too late, she kissed him and gave him a present. Now he could breathe. She passed her hands over her eyes, damaging her make-up.

Her companion this evening was Etienne, whose real name was Steven. He was an American boy who had left Michigan for a while to live in Paris with his French mother. The mother was generous with money, allowing Etienne to pursue his calling as a non-speaking actor in French films. He looked very good kissing a girl in the street in the name of background colour, or sitting significantly at a café table. He pretended that this was all he wanted to do and her heart had gone out to him because of the humiliation he had absorbed. She had taken up with him at first because he was pretty but also because he was neurotic enough to be diverting. When Etienne was overcast, Nerida became breezy. Their clashing

62

moods generated enough drama to keep the liaison lively, on tenterhooks, and this mutual feinting passed for love. Tonight though, Nerida observed that Etienne was not as good-looking as he had seemed to be at lunch. He had begun to find self-pity irresistible.

On the stage a dwarf dressed in a crinoline rose and fell on a swing whose ropes were garlanded with paper roses. The curtain had hoisted on this *fête galante* as a picnic was ending. Aristocratic women, their breasts exposed, spurned their men in a sudden unexplained display of pouting and foot-stamping and then began to make love to one another. The excess of prettiness made Nerida feel bad-tempered. Everything was white and pink and pale green. She thought of iced cakes, the kind that cry eat-me, eat-me, and then later make you feel sick and manic. Slender hands slid up powdered thighs, brushing taffeta skirts aside, persuading legs to part. But Nerida, who sat near the lip of the stage, observed that flesh never touched flesh.

Since lunchtime, several events had occurred. She knew a dresser at Chanel whose brother taught film at a university. At a party she had been masochistically enthralled by his condescending conversation, thick with theory and interpretation, and by his passionless delivery. She had stood there like an ornament made of glass. You could see right through her. Her erotic aura, in the past so powerful and prophylactic, had been neutralised by his command of words. Nerida wondered afterwards why this should be so. Worse than neutralised. He'd dug a pit with his erudition and filled it with spikes and laid bracken over the top. Being too stupid to avoid this snare, she had fallen in and languished.

Then today, after lunch, walking through the Place des Invalides, she had experienced a sense of absence so acute she'd had to pause to catch her breath. In order to rise above, it was necessary to capture facts, to master a subject. Then you would possess a trophy called knowledge. Knowledge endured. A shift took place in the lightweight thing she thought of as her mind. The mind as a fine-mesh garment, easily divested in order to reveal the real thing of substance: the body. She was standing on the deck of the departing ship watching the streamers tear and then fall into the churning water.

An hour later when she tried to insert the key into the lock of Etienne's apartment, it would not fit. She forced it to no avail. At that moment Monsieur Pitault, a small dentist who lived on the floor above, appeared on the landing and murmured, 'Excuse me, but I believe you have the wrong apartment.'

Feeling foolish, Nerida thanked him and turned to mount the stairs. Seizing her hand, the dentist pressed it against his crotch. There was nothing there but thick folds of woollen fabric. Then he leaned closer and licked her cheek with the tip of his tongue.

'You are a very stupid girl,' he said. Releasing her, he pattered down the stairs.

As the curtain dropped to sporadic applause, Etienne ordered another two bottles of champagne at fantastic expense, although the tableaux were almost at an end. They had already witnessed Ste Thérèse in ecstasy with a supernatural being, a footman's contribution to Marie Antoinette's last night at Varennes, and a gymnastic routine between Leda and the swan. Saxophonic music, sexual tension and miasmic conversation seeped through the club like a narcotic gas that fucked your judgement. A wavering woman, trying to squeeze between the stage and a chair, spilled her green drink, a grasshopper, on Nerida's white lace dress. Everybody except Nerida shrugged. Etienne was suddenly very drunk. Pouring champagne on a napkin, he began to wipe her dress.

Nerida gazed at Queen Christina leaving her homeland, cloaked and proud at the prow of her ship, her throne abandoned for the sake of love. Dry ice and violins encouraged the queen's mood of lonely resolution. She wore scarlet glitter on her lips. She raised her arms so the wind machine could blow back the cloak. Her breasts were fugitive but their nipples were large and rouged. She slithered on to the figurehead, a mermaid, of her ship.

Etienne had ceased to dab at Nerida's stain. She saw that he had become bored and angry. Poor baby, oppressed by his beautiful face – although he hadn't realised that. Etienne was hardly ever required to exercise his mind. Nerida thought that his dark moods were the only means he had of proving his existence. The kind of women who might have made something of him, women older than she, more stabilised, could not see past his appearance. He was a fuck, not a lover. After all, they thought, he's a boy who could only love himself. Perched on the edge of a stagnant pool.

Nerida had only come to know him because she had been recuperating from a bout of anaemia at his sister's apartment, a place that Etienne regarded as a refuge when depression overtook him. From the moment she saw him, she found his susceptibility to despair to be alluring. She had found his weakness. Her weakness, which he never discovered, was Narcissus.

Abandoning Le Jaguar, Nerida and Etienne wandered to the kerb. Etienne swayed, putting his hand on her shoulder to balance himself. He was too cool to hold her hand. He thought it didn't matter. He craved both proximity and distance. He was a mess.

'Let's go someplace else. I hate that dive.' He was surveying the street for a cab.

'I'm going to walk back to the hotel.'

'It's fucking miles. Don't be so stupid.'

65

Nerida raised her hand, attracting the attention of a taxi. Opening the door, Etienne motioned her to get in. Nerida shook her head. Etienne flung himself into the car and slammed the door. She had mistaken, previously, his petulance for the grandeur of despair. Bye-bye, baby. The taxi took off, and in the morning another taxi would deliver him to a movie set where he would pretend to kiss the girl.

Nerida walked on. The cafés were putting up their shutters. It was the time of night when people became unattractive, drunk, disorderly, like that crowd there outside a restaurant, belligerent with lack of resolution. It was miles to the hotel and she didn't want to walk alone with her thoughts. She wanted to read magazines and assert herself as a frivolous, beautiful creature floating free of anything truly painful or piercing. A cab idled at the kerb and automatically Nerida climbed wearily into it. The driver looked taken aback, but when she gave the address of her hotel he said with irritation, 'Yeah, yeah, I know. Rue de l'Université.' Appraising the stain on her dress, he made no move to put the car into gear. Then the door opened and a tall man climbed in, holding a fresh newspaper.

'She's here,' said the driver, jerking his head in Nerida's direction. Slamming his foot on the accelerator, he penetrated the late-night traffic. Nerida and the interloper exchanged remarks of surprise and apology. Both offered to abandon the taxi until it was established that he too was staying at the Lenox in rue de l'Université. They drove to their destination in silence and then shared the cost.

Inside the Lenox they shook hands, formally. He looked like a photograph taken by Edward Weston in 1924 of Manuel Hernández Galván, shooting. Latino, maybe. Olive skin. Exceptional hands. Good shirt. She liked him very much, which was, she told herself, not worth much.

'Good-night,' he said in English. 'Sleep well.'

66

The unexpected English sounded intimate. She needn't have bothered with French in the taxi. They could have spoken their own language.

'Thank you,' she smiled. 'But I always do.'

He returned the smile and then his eyes focused on her mouth. 'Where are you from?'

'London.'

He stared at her hard. 'And originally?'

She made a wiping motion with her hand. 'Somewhere distant.' A potentially huge, possibly eternal conversation swirled around them, unspoken; but to have a drink together or a coffee at an hour when drinks were consumed to lubricate sexual encounters seemed an expression of banality that would have embarrassed them both. They parted with reluctance.

9

In the Café-Zar, Nerida had chosen a table against a far wall where she could load her camera away from the flare of the sun. She did not notice Alexis Serafin enter the café, but, against her will, she was thinking about him. She'd enjoyed the silence between them during the ride to the Lenox. Without speaking, he seemed to have spoken to her for hours. When he had shaken her hand in the foyer, her body had shuddered as if two interlocking mechanisms had forcefully engaged, dovetailing into a tight, enduring fit. This sensation of gut-rooted, fateful inevitability filled her with apprehension.

She'd woken several times in the night, comforted to find the room dark, the bed warm. In the morning she dressed with care. She filed her fingernails. Walking through the Lenox's foyer, she decided to have her hair cut, immediately, and was directed to a salon a block away where she took advantage of a cancelled appointment. Since Nerida had withdrawn from modelling, it no longer mattered how she constructed her appearance. Now her hair was less blonde. Positioned between two mirrors, the one behind held by the judgemental, elderly hairdresser who had seen a thousand transformations in her time, Nerida turned her head slowly from side to side, watching the light play on her face. She seemed alternately to be older and younger. Her newly revealed neck and ears looked vulnerable. The hairdresser, finally unpursing her magenta lips, complimented Nerida on the shape of her skull.

Nerida placed the exposed film in her bag and wound on the new film. Thirty-six exposures of Etienne, who loved being photographed, as she had once done, to check that he was still alive. She was relieved to be free of him. She could now believe her life to be virgin and blank, detached from men and all their jealousies and assertions. Men were only mirrors. She gazed into them and sometimes a trick of the light made her look like a woman in love.

Nerida intended to drift from place to place, protected from disappointment and frustration by a complete lack of ambition. The camera would accompany her everywhere but more as a cipher than a serious instrument of art. Art was dangerous. She had seen it lead to hubris and the combustion of volatile personalities. She intended to soak in a long vacation from the imposition of will, her own as well as that of others. This aimlessness ought to have marked her as a weak and superficial human being, another uselessly decorative girl in a city of decorative girls, but the struggle that took place within Nerida to sustain this pose, a struggle scarcely acknowledged by herself except for isolated moments such as those in the Place des Invalides when she was reprimanded by her intelligence, this produced an air of complexity, a suggestion of depth, despite her jewellery and make-up, which lent her singularity. That, and the impression that she was comfortable with her own company. She did not seek applause. Nerida peered through the viewfinder, killing time, and thought about ordering another coffee.

At the bar, Alexis was trying to catch the eye of the counterman. Although he had almost two free days in Paris before leaving for a conference in Geneva, Alexis was in a hurry. Constantin Leonte was expecting him, although there was every possibility that Constantin would forget their appointment if he had been working through the night. Then he could be found in any bar in Belleville, drinking his first *pastis* of the day, exercising his talent for self-destruction. Alexis enjoyed, and was also disturbed by, Constantin's thoughtless romanticism. If Constantin was not home, no doubt Alexis would be unearthed by Eugene Rinehart whose usually anodyne company became unacceptable here. Paris did not bring out the best in him. Its gilded cultural superiority made Eugene angry and insecure, predisposing him to *faux pas*.

Nerida glanced around her to catch the attention of a waiter and saw Alexis Serafin standing at the bar with his back to her, failing to place his order. The counterman was occupied elaborately wiping up a minor puddle of coffee adjacent to the cup of a young woman.

Look my way. Now. No. Don't look my way.

Shrugging, Alexis turned and gazed into the recesses of the café. The pretty, dishevelled woman who had shared his taxi the previous evening was sitting at a far table holding a camera to her chest. She had a stunned expression on her face as if a catastrophe had occurred. He was startled to see that her hair had been cut. Because around dawn he had awoken from a dream in which she read a book at his desk, her head bent forward. He had taken a small pair of scissors and snipped at her hair until the nape of her neck was exposed. She had let him do it. Her hair fell on to the pages. Depositing the camera with a clunk on to the table, she pushed her chair back, the iron legs jarring on the wooden floor.

She had been waiting for him.

He crossed the room and indicated one of the chairs at her table with an enquiring look.

'Of course. Please sit down.'

He placed the flat of his hand against his head. 'It suits you.'

She nodded. 'Are you in a hurry?' She seemed anxious, as if seeing him were the worst thing in the world.

'Not at all.'

The waiter materialised and they ordered coffee. She began playing with the sugar bowl, pleating a paper napkin. He too felt absurdly on edge, alienated from his normal personality, as if he were experiencing the onset of a trance. He reminded himself that he was a man who held audiences in the palm of his hand. His hands were tingling now. He wished he and Nerida were meeting in a dimly lit bar after several drinks. When the waiter brought their espressos, Nerida drank hers all at once. Alexis concluded, to his keen disappointment, that she wanted to leave as soon as possible. His skin burned. He was lying stranded and light-headed on his bed, flung there by the force of a detonation as a result of reading *NarZiss*. She sat at his bedside and laid her cool hand on his forehead. There was an unfinished conversation or a conversation not yet begun. He wanted to seize her wrist to detain her, and then begin speaking.

As Nerida crashed her empty cup into its saucer, she felt she had wrought a terrible conclusion to this encounter. Be calm. I am drinking a cup of coffee with a meaningless stranger. In a minute he will finish his coffee and leave. She stared distractedly at the windows, seeking intervention. Then the sun disappeared and it began suddenly to rain.

'It's raining,' Alexis said with relief.

Now she smiled. I'm perverse, my head full of wild thoughts. I caught a cab all the way across town to meet you here, miserable until I saw you and could lay my hands on your glowing flesh. I've never slept with anybody before, I'm sure of it. Didn't I leave you a surfeit of messages and call your number endlessly wondering why you never answered? That is my instantaneous feeling. Those are the things I wanted to do. 'What are you doing in Paris?'

He laughed. 'Enjoying the Bohemian life.'

'So am I. Whatever that is.'

'It concerns a person of loose and irregular habits. My father was one, an actual Bohemian I mean. It's a sort of joke place to be from, like Transylvania or something. But my mother was English.' He wondered why he had suddenly lurched on to the subject of his parents. Snap out of it, Alexis. You must be very tired. Thinking about Geneva and Karcevskij and Papa and the terror of never amounting to anything.

'Was it a good combination? Their nationalities?'

'I've spent years trying to work that out. He was drawn to the phlegmatic English thing, I think to discipline himself. But my mother was anything but phlegmatic. May I ask you something?'

She nodded. A strand of hair fell over her forehead. He checked the impulse to brush it back.

'Where are you from?'

'You already asked me that.'

'And you said, London.'

She sat back in her chair with a challenging look. Which drove him to ostentation: 'There's this anti-cadence in your voice – '

'An anti-cadence? That sounds technical.'

'I'm a linguist,' he said helplessly, thinking: Is that supposed to be impressive?

Her smile was sweet and beautiful, emphasising her cheek-bones. 'Then I guess I should watch what I say. Do you teach at a university?'

'From time to time. But basically I'm free to do as I like.'

'Me too. I drift.'

He tapped the camera. 'What about this?'

'The usual tourist accessory. It's just for fun. Tell me some more about your father.'

Alexis smiled and shook his head. 'I hardly know you. You want to hear about my father?'

'You introduced him. The Bohemian. There must be something to say.'

'Yes, I did. I don't know why. You make me nervous, Nerida, which is not my usual condition.'

'You make me nervous, Alexis. Which is why I'm interested in hearing about a third party.'

'It's not very entertaining. I'll sound like I'm giving a lecture.'

Nerida placed her hands, palms open, on the table. 'That's fine. I like being lectured. It's relaxing.'

I tear open her dress and place my mouth on her breast. Then I lie down on the ground beside her chair. My hand grips her ankle. 'Why do you think that woman over there is drinking whisky with her cake?'

Nerida followed his gaze. A middle-aged, immaculately dressed bourgeoise, wearing heavy make-up to conceal the puffiness of her eyes, was compulsively devouring a rum baba, while gulping at a glass of Scotch. A cigarette burned in her ashtray.

'She's hell-bent on comforting herself. Something's really upset her.'

The café began to fill with damp patrons escaping the rain. Voices hummed and burbled. The smell of ham and cheese and coffee suggested that appetites were about to be satisfied. Knives and forks clinked on thick, unbreakable china. Nerida and Alexis began to feel less alone.

Alexis said, 'Do you want something to eat? You look hungry.'

'No, no. I don't want anything. Thank you. I used to be a model. We always look hungry.'

'I thought you were very elegantly dressed for a drifter.'

'Maybe traveller is a better description.'

73

'You're from New Zealand, I think.'

Nerida inclined her head and puckered up her face. 'Yes, I am.'

'I am too. I grew up in Auckland.'

Her mouth fell open. 'You did? That's really hard to believe.' She laughed while feeling inwardly disappointed. She did not want to be reminded of New Zealand because she had not been successful there. On the other hand, he too seemed to have obliterated his past. His accent was impeccably English. She waved her slender hand in the air. 'Your disguise is completely convincing.'

Alexis grinned. 'For years my parents coached me in suave European ways. Where did you grow up?'

Nerida stared at the woman near by who was sopping up the remains of the rum syrup in her plate. 'Up north, you know, surrounded by animals. That's it. I left when I was nineteen. Was your father a linguist too?'

Alexis let himself be deflected. Her refusal to exclaim over the coincidence of their being from the same country appealed to him. He liked her restraint. 'Oh yes, but he was a terrible faker.'

Nerida leaned forward slightly, with an enquiring expression, encouraging him to continue.

Alexis took a deep breath. He'd never discussed this aspect of his father out loud before and it seemed injudicious to be doing it now. But amazingly, he could think of no other topic of conversation. 'For a long time, we didn't realise how bitter he was. For a long time he impersonated a scholar. But by the time I was fourteen or fifteen, I would read the things he published – never books, although he was always apparently working on one . . . At first they were essays in various reviews and journals, but later just comments and notes. They became increasingly caustic. I think my mother – I mean I adored her – but in a way she dissipated Papa's concentration.

74

He couldn't finish anything, probably because he was always talking to her about what he should have been writing, and then they'd stop for drinks or a meal or a holiday or any other distraction. So he made up for it as he got older and past really achieving anything by writing a fusillade of retorts and denunciations and amendments . . . There's nothing worse, you know, than potential unfulfilled. Basically he was writing a big advertisement for his resentment at having a defunct career. People – scholars – got sick of the sight of his name. There's an excess of words there – which is a souvenir of my childhood. My father and I had a lot of interaction with dictionaries. When I think of him thousands of meanings spring to mind. Thousands of words.'

'You're fortunate to have so many at your disposal. I get by on glances and gestures most of the time.'

'Women seem to be very fluent in glances and gestures. My mother and my sister were both very good at speaking volumes without opening their mouths.'

'And what happened to him?'

The waiter returned with lunch menus, which Nerida and Alexis placed carefully on the table without looking at them.

'Oh, a downhill slide. A declining reputation. He tried to prop it up by going in for a sort of bilious linguistic journalism. The kind of thing that appeals to recent graduates and second-rate scholars. They identified their own grievances in his criticism. But no one of any real worth took him seriously. Finally he had a stroke. For about a year he staggered around with a stick. He could speak but his memory was shot. He couldn't read. Anyway, you think: That's what education does for you. You come to find yourself fascinating; others less so.'

'What about your mother?'

Alexis felt suddenly irate; an emotion that he suppressed

75

abruptly, but not before Nerida, to her consternation, noticed a closed expression come over his face.

'She died within the year. One hoped that she would live longer.' He had said too much.

Nerida cursed herself for causing an embarrassment when she had meant to go straight to the heart of him. She was hopeless at small-talk. 'I'm sorry to hear that,' she said.

Loathing his vanity, Alexis withdrew money from his wallet, replaced the wallet in his breast pocket and buttoned his jacket conclusively.

'I must go, but thank you for your company,' he said with a serene, practised smile. 'I'm travelling to Geneva in the morning. A conference.'

Nerida shrugged. Something had gone wrong and she was powerless to prevent his departure. She watched him disappear into the drizzle. As she vacated the table she felt the gaze of her whisky-drinking neighbour on her. The woman gave Nerida a sardonic smile, as if they shared the same sour secret.

10

'Alexis! Hey, monster! Kiss me!' But Constantin kissed Alexis first, his lips smacking juicily on both cheeks, his torso crushing the bouquet of irises that Alexis held. Then he took Alexis's free hand and dragged him into the apartment. Alexis was delighted to be led. The apartment belonged to Constantin's American wife Linda, who brought home all the bacon. It was scarcely larger than a studio, Linda having preferred to sacrifice space for an address in a good *arrondissement*. Constantin's desk, which had been a dining table in a former life, bore all the signs of an extended cerebral frenzy. Books, stationery, ashtrays and two empty wine bottles lay strewn, exhausted, on its surface. The atmosphere in the apartment was close, oppressive, swarming with latent ideas. Opening a window, Constantin let them out. His eyes were swollen, his face unshaven. He was barefoot. He beamed at Alexis.

'Very, very wonderful to see you, Alexis.' He flicked at invisible dust on Alexis's lapel. 'You're looking like a smart man.'

'And you are looking relaxed.'

Constantin made a floppy movement with his arms as if they were made of rubber. 'I'm as happy as a large dog.'

Constantin was not troubled by aspiration. He wrote and drank, he slept, he spent hours shooting the breeze. He looked like a manual labourer with his stocky body, a yellow Gitane hanging from his lip and a *ballon* of red wine in his hand. Alexis saw in him an extreme example of himself, which was an affirmation, since Constantin was an antidote to the bloodlessness of academe, but also a warning.

Alexis waved the irises. 'These are for Linda. I'm sorry I missed her.'

'She's sorry too. But, you know, she runs here, she runs there. She's got American energy.' Constantin seized the irises and then, as he was unfamiliar with the location of vases, laid the bouquet on the sofa-bed. The flowers seemed suddenly funereal to Alexis, but Constantin patted them with satisfaction and returned to the kitchen. Hopefully Linda would return before they were completely dead and introduce them to water. Constantin scratched his stomach. 'Nice day, yes? Birds and sunshine.' He made loud chirping noises at the sparrows hopping on the windowsill. They panicked and flew away. 'You've brought your paper, I hope? What's your topic?'

'Zeugen's Phonologic Representation.'

'I see. OK. That's good. I'll read it.'

'I'd like you to. I want your opinion.'

Constantin's mouth made a deprecating plosive sound, then he hitched his trousers. 'But first, coffee. To aid the digestion.' He squinted at the kitchen bench, looking helpless. Making a phonological analysis: as easy as falling off a bar stool. But making a cup of coffee, that was demanding, if not impossible.

Linda managed Constantin, she organised him, since he was so vague about practical matters he could hardly tie his own shoelaces. This was the result of an upbringing in which his parents, ambitious for their scintillating son, had arranged his life so that he might give full attention to his books. In doing so, they had removed all motivation from him for anything except the desire to escape his family. This he had done by winning a scholarship to write his doctoral thesis in France, leaving Romania behind for ever. The thesis had never been completed although Alexis considered Constantin to be brilliant. But his mind was also a circus, with one dizzy thing happening after another. Acrobats and trapeze artists tumbled and swung, animals leapt through flaming hoops, while clowns capered in the sawdust, causing mock explosions. After the show they all went out for a few drinks.

Leaving Alexis to make the coffee, Constantin selected a Liszt concerto from his small record collection and when the music began, he took up the paper that Alexis was to deliver in Geneva. He stared at the title page for a minute or so then heaved himself on to the bench next to Alexis. Constantin radiated warmth.

'So finally you declare your interest in Zeugen. This is a good moment for you.'

'What do you mean?'

'I don't give a fuck about this career thing and this reputation thing. You know that. I've always been outside the window and that's what I like. But you, you've got one foot in and one foot out. Right now everything sparkles. Everything with Dr Serafin is very kinetic.'

'But . . .'

'You tell me what the "but" is.'

'I'm thinking, Constantin, that I've had it very easy. I write on everything.' The coffee began to spurt. For a second Alexis thought of telling Constantin about his epileptic condition, about his miraculously assisted ability. No one, apart from Moorgate, knew of it. Alexis had not even revealed the inflation of this phenomenon to Drusilla, although there had once been a time when they shared everything. He had not told anyone because in his heart he felt ashamed, as if he had seized an unfair advantage and could not fairly claim credit for his achievements. Also, he was inspired during his psychotronic episodes to attack any linguistic theme, to analyse any aspect, but as time passed, he considered that his work, although discretely dazzling, lacked consistency. It lacked a vision. It was only chemical. Alexis poured the coffee. When he asked Constantin for the sugar, Constantin could not remember where it was kept. Alexis found it in a canister marked 'Sugar'.

'The thing is, I'm promiscuous.'

Constantin laughed. 'It happens.'

'And I'm starting to think I've got a disease. It's spelled: dilettante. I think my time as a youthful prodigy is running out. I'm thirty. I'm looking sideways at myself.'

'Write more on Zeugen. Nobody cares about him. He's out of the limelight. He was a lush and nobody likes that. Not lush as in – ' Constantin made a drinking motion and then reached for the Spanish cognac which he splashed into his coffee. 'You could make the rescue. There were accusations of soulfulness. Poor Zeugen. Well? You have something to say?'

'I feel like I'm standing outside a magnificent but gloomy piece of architecture. I'm swinging through the piazza on my way to a jazz club where some woman is waiting for me and I pass by this enormous basilica. I like the look of it. I want to go in because it's a thrilling monument. It's solid and so sincere it's transcendental. But if I do, my mood will change. I'll feel serious and conscious of my own meagreness. And afterwards the jazz will sound tinny and the conversation will be pointless and the sex will be insipid. And I'll feel aimless and depressed. That is not like me at all. I think *joie de vivre* is an excellent thing. I like to carry some with me at all times, especially for use in an emergency such as a sudden attack of introspection.' Alexis held up his hand. 'Don't say anything. Just read the paper.'

Constantin took the manuscript and stretched out on the couch. Alexis lounged on the wide windowsill and let the

sun fall on his face. Nerida. He wished he had not been so
intimate – no, not intimate, just pathetic. He had not taken
her in hand as was his custom. It was strange that she was
from New Zealand. Because, like him, she didn't seem to be.
Romanians like Constantin, on the other hand, Jewish boys
like Eugene Rinehart, they carried their culture with them.
And then he noticed a beaded strip hanging on the far wall,
in a pattern of Xs.

'Constantin? Is this from Drusilla?' Alexis strode across the
room and examined the textile.

'The hatband? Yes. She sent it from Jalisco. She has sent
something like that to you?'

'No. She doesn't write.'

'But you are close, yes?'

'We are close. It doesn't matter about the writing.'

Constantin sat up. 'I could have loved her.'

'Drusilla?'

'You sent her to me.'

'Well not on an amorous mission.'

'I could have loved her and left Linda and done the whole
thing. But her heart is shut. She is so beautiful, you know?
To see that woman is to want to put your tongue in her mouth
and also suck out her brains because she's secretive and that's
a big sex thing.'

'It's weird to hear you talk like this about Drusilla.'

Constantin slumped back into his reading position. 'So
don't talk about her. I spread myself on the floor. She said
no. I drank numerous litres of wine until she was gone.'

'I never knew this.'

'Why should you know? What? You have some contract?
You're the brother but it's not Africa. It's not Latin America.
OK, Monsieur Anthropologist. May I read this Zeugen now?
Maybe with music louder?'

'You may.' Alexis increased the volume, wondering how

81

Constantin could concentrate over the desperate orchestra. But Constantin had hardly read the first page of Alexis's paper before he began enthusiastically to add and amend, saliva flecking his moustache, his hand dashing the air for emphasis.

Nerida's interlude with Alexis Serafin had effected a transitory vexation in her but, characteristically, she refused to capitulate to it. She had spent the afternoon photographing tourists in the Bois de Boulogne. Then she had mailed the undeveloped films, as she always did, to her agency address in London. Huge numbers of the canisters were accumulating but this did not concern her. She was satisfied by small actions: the loading of the film, the click of the shutter, the trip to the post office, the visit to an airline where she randomly bought a ticket to Mexico. She would leave in two days' time after paying a couple of courtesy calls on acquaintances. She valued good manners.

The receptionist at the Lenox handed her several messages, all of them requiring the use of her face and her body. Her booker had made the receptionist copy down an exhortation: 'Last Chance!' This only increased Nerida's refusal to reply to them.

As she stepped out of the lift on the second floor, she saw Alexis applying his key to a room not far from her own. He looked up sharply, although her footsteps had made no sound on the thick carpet. She raised her hand, more in a salute than a wave. Leaving the key dangling in the lock, he took a step towards her. They greeted one another politely. They said: How are you? How are you? I'm fine. I'm very well. Do you often stay at this hotel? I like it. I like this street. So do I. The Lutetia is good too. I've always liked art deco. I was bad company this morning. That's fine. It's just some kind of nervousness, you don't know where it comes from.

Alexis was surprised to hear this. 'Nervousness? That makes me sound like a racehorse.'

'Or something. I wondered what was so important about Geneva.'

'I'm not going to mention my father again. You already know enough to write a biography.'

'What will you talk about in Geneva?'

'A man called Samuel Zeugen.'

'Z-e-u-g-e-n?'

'You know of him?'

'No. I suppose he had an unhappy life.'

'I can't decide about that.'

'I can't stand the glamour of unhappiness.'

When she said that, her voice calm and coldly determined, he wanted to sit her down on a hard-backed chair and interrogate her about everything that had happened in her life. He wanted to tell her everything that had happened in his. Nerida opened her mouth. She was about to add something. He wanted to hear whatever she had to say. A bell sounded as the lift doors slid open and an American accent called out, 'Lexie!' A sudden shower passed overhead.

Nerida and Alexis read disappointment in one another's faces as a short man bounced towards them. Anyway, Nerida thought, he leaves for Geneva tomorrow.

'Eugene. You've tracked me down.'

'Good luck,' Nerida whispered. Fleetingly, Alexis put his hand on her arm. But Nerida fled before she could be introduced to the interloper with his round cheerful face and flapping clothes.

11

Nerida lay on her bed for half an hour, planning her evening. She was expected at Patrick Paquin's cocktail party. Yes. It was very necessary to go out for a drink. Her heartbeat fluctuated as someone rapped on her door. She walked slowly to the door and pulled it open. A maid stood there holding her white lace dress in a plastic wrapper, drycleaned. It gave Nerida great pleasure to step into this dress and with supple movements pull the zip closed so that she looked exactly as she had the evening before, only stainless.

She didn't hail a cab at once. She walked, even though her shoes were unsuitable for the hard streets. She walked until she chanced upon an English-language bookshop. Its customers glanced at her curiously, a woman wearing a cocktail dress and jewellery, purposefully searching the shelves. In a History of Anthropology series, she found a long essay on Samuel Zeugen.

She was suddenly hungry. Carrying the book in her hand, she wandered into a crêperie in rue Grégoire de Tours, a student place with high ceilings, smoked walls, long wooden tables and a pleasantly fervent atmosphere. Craving something sweet, she ordered a crêpe smothered in a purée of marrons glacés flavoured with rum. Happily, she opened the book. At first she found the essay indigestible, as dry as a biscuit, but as she persevered, even the flat, declarative prose did not prevent Samuel

Zeugen from engaging her sympathies and then her retiring intellect.

Although described generally as an anthropologist, it was Zeugen's linguistic abilities, his flair for structure, that made his name. He was an American of Austrian extraction who had come to prominence in the twenties at Columbia University where he was a student of Frank Boas. He experienced a distinguished career culminating in his great work on North American Indian culture, published in 1933, titled *Time, Truth and Language*. Zeugen asked if there was such a thing as unified culture; or were there only fragments conditioned by changing contexts? He investigated the linguistic expression of cultural patterns in order to expose their structures.

Zeugen believed that intuition and emotion construct those patterns that synthesise the splintered psyche, and he wrote like that. He brought a passionate analysis to bear on the science of linguistics. He balanced form with feeling. His work manifested his personality. Nerida sipped from her bowl of cider. Cider. Normandy. Chanel had a wild time there with her lover. Structuralism was the means by which Zeugen pursued the place of the helplessly subjective individual. There was still time to go to the party before she did something extreme. But she felt compelled to finish the essay.

In 1934 Zeugen reached a turning point. He published *NarZiss*, a collection of poetry in which he explored the tension between lyric poetry as the poetry of the first person and epic poetry as the poetry of the third, for those disposed to literary analysis. But the words that leapt off the page for any sentient person to understand, any gas station attendant or student or sales assistant or model if they were not watching television, were words of desire and frustration. This attempt to mythologise the personal attracted scathing reviews and accusations of self-absorption. At the end of that year, Zeugen's wife committed suicide.

Two years later, Zeugen took leave from his university post and travelled to Ireland where he based himself in Sligo. His wife's family had come from there. Living alone in a leaking farmhouse, he completed two works. The first, *Great Time and the Holy Beginning*, was a study of Celtic story-telling in which he cleaved to familiar, some even said obsessive, themes. External reality is shaped by the accusing finger. The individual is trapped in a nexus of self-imposed laws and interdicts, which accuse and accuse and wrap him in guilt. This is insupportable. So this individual weaves a cocoon around himself and inside this shroud, he comes to know himself. He is transformed by self-knowledge and in time emerges to take charge of the world. *Great Time*, while acknowledged by Zeugen's critics to be a perceptive, empathetic work, was generally judged to be embarrassingly corrupted by his private life.

As he became preoccupied by poetry, Zeugen's professional, technical output began to shrivel. He dedicated a second collection of poems to his wife, which was only fitfully reviewed. Depressed by political events in Europe, he returned home. Despite his shadowy state of mind, his lectures were still considered incisive and inspiring. Nerida turned to the photograph at the front of the book. She saw a middle-aged man with a receding hairline and a tendency to jowliness. But he possessed a sensuous, well-shaped mouth and beneath the deep lines raking his forehead, very dark eyes. He did not look terminal, but who could tell? You pay the rent, you chat to a friend, you drive the car, you cook scrambled eggs, you give incisive, inspiring lectures and live with despair.

When the United States entered the war, Samuel Zeugen, to the surprise of his colleagues, volunteered for the army. He was posted to the Pacific. On leave in Auckland in 1944, he disappeared. He was discovered one month later, washed up in a bay in the far north of New Zealand. The gunshot wound in the right temple was judged to have been self-inflicted. When the inquest was held, his journals were offered as chief evidence of his mental instability.

Nerida's mind jumped at seeing the name of her country, so rarely uttered or read in the world. Unable to remain in the restaurant for a moment longer, she finished her second bowl of cider and closed the critical study. She was required elsewhere. Returning to her hotel room, she sat in an uncomfortable chair, the Zeugen book burning in her hand. She would have liked to banish fervour and desire, those blowsy emotions that hauled you on to the dance floor even when you were really tired and just wanted to go home. Sex and pseudo-love. Like that girl who had to dance in red-hot shoes until she died.

She watched herself pick up the telephone and ask to speak to Monsieur Serafin. He had not yet come in. An hour passed, during which she lay on the bed with her eyes open while the published thoughts of Samuel Zeugen swam through her head:

At the surface the current is relatively fast.
Only certain wave movements in the bay outline the tide.
Drift renders innocuous by washing the old significance out.
Spirit.
Impulse.
Craving.

Nerida went out into the street to wait for Alexis Serafin, pacing in front of the hotel, not caring what the staff thought. When his taxi arrived, she ran to the door as he was opening it. She ran with a friendly smile on her face as if they had arranged to meet and it seemed to him that they had. Taking her hand, he helped her into the cab, asking the driver to drive some distance, perhaps to Porte de Clichy.

Nerida kissed him as hard as she could. He tasted of wine and his tongue was slick. Her kiss was sudden and aggressive. His eyes had been fixed on a leaf of paper but now she turned his head to the left and sank her teeth into his neck. Alexis believed he saw flashes of light, street lights, neon, dancing on the cusp of his vision. Something was dying to burst out of him. Nerida kept on kissing him, her fingers pressed against his face. His chest was heaving. As she changed position, straddling his thighs, she displaced a manila folder that had been lying on the seat. Papers fell everywhere. She started again, forcing his head against the seat. He was drinking up the kiss, trying to raise his head to her. But she pushed him down, tightening her knees against his hips, ignoring the driver who ignored them.

Alexis was disoriented. The world erased. She had taken his breath away. Nerida was relentless even when he began to make strange noises in his throat as if he were trying to project a groan, a scream. She hung over his face. The soft, suffocating earth. And then a vaporous apparition rose out of a dark place to meet him. He put his hands on her shoulders, slid his hands down to hold her breasts. He clutched at them, not stroking or doing anything tender, squeezing each breast so hard that it hurt. Her tongue ached and her lips felt swollen. She moved her fingers on to his throat. He was shaking. His carotid artery pulsed with blood. She could feel a pulse in his erection. She sighed, letting her breath escape into his mouth and then released him from her mouth.

'Alexis . . .'

He threw back his head, sucking in a great draught of air. She tore at his belt, unzipped him and grasped his cock. When he came he uttered unintelligible words. Nerida was wedged between the seats, on the floor of the cab, her head between his legs. He pulled her on to the seat next to him and kissed her face. He held her hand.

'What happened?'

He wanted to tell her that a genie had come out of a cave.

Later that night in the Hotel Lenox. Early the following morning in the Hotel Lenox. He reared up, kneeling on the end of the bed, his penis an arrow aimed at her. Everything else about his body tender and smooth. She wanted to take that thing in her mouth but not yet. It was good to look at. A definition of desire. Just looking at it caused a tug between her legs, liquid forming. You couldn't tell what she was thinking, lying there, even though her eyes weren't closed. Now I'm focused. Now I'm dispersed. Her hands weren't on him. She lay there like a target.

His blood rushed, his body flew through the air towards her. If someone came running into the room shouting 'Fire!' he wouldn't be able to deflect himself from her.

He didn't do anything, didn't touch her, but she was already imagining it, wanted to writhe and sigh. At first he had been far away. Now he was coming closer. She looked desperately at his hands, his fingers – even one finger on her, dragging lightly along her thigh, would be a totality. Desire concertinaed, telescoped, compressed, detailed in the most fleeting contact; the kind you could have any time in everyday life, a friend laying a hand on your shoulder, a colleague shaking your hand, a passerby even . . . and none of it had the collapsing intensity of this moment now. Touch me. Please. Brush your fingers against. Thinking of rain and grass and wet sand and any stupid thing so that you're straining at the expectation of something as dumb and elusive as happiness.

I'm going to touch her. She's so soft. Like butter. Like fur. Her wet mouth. Her teeth. He crouched over her and began to kiss her. He swiped his tongue over her mouth like I'm not even really kissing you, it's just vast merging, liquid mingling, I can't concentrate on this because I'm going to do it now. That was easy. Now I'm inside you. You're very syrupy, you're sweet and your breasts and your hips and your throat are . . . no words now . . .

A surge, that's what it is. I don't think he can tell from the outside because I haven't said anything. I can't speak because of the sensation of that packed flesh filling up *me* . . . I'll – He's doing this slow, I like it slow. How can he stay in there and open me up at the same time I get this tight feeling, essential tight, prickling, flickering, now I can't keep my hands on, move them on to his back, fingernails, teeth. He's going to stop, no he's still going, everything's sliding the bed the ceiling the sheets our bodies. It's hot in here. This is happening fast now, this is a dance, this is ludicrous, this is incredible, I don't know what to do with my hands. I want to grip his shoulders, I want to fling my arms wide on the bed, I want to tangle them in his hair. My mouth opens. Stays open. I cry.

He gasps, he shudders, he holds her so tight she can hardly breathe. He sighs and falling out of her he reaches down and strokes, strokes her. She starts to tremble again. She presses herself against him very hard to ground that electricity, that lightning bolt.

12

Nerida and Alexis were in accord, which is to say that their separate identities had morphed into a single being whose name was Delight. They could have practised irony and distance, but they did not wish to be barbarians or to be fatuous. They did not marry but they agreed on food, humour, movies, clothes, architecture and interior design, landscapes, models of cars, indifference to weather, fragrances, art, stationery, manners, television programmes, toiletries, newspapers, music and brands of appliances. In the area of taste and discrimination, neither offered any resistance, appreciating their mutual confidence and experience.

They shared an appearance. Slender, attenuated bodies and strong faces. The same and the reverse. The same chocolate-coloured eyes. The same prominent mouths and fine, flopping hair. The same bony wrists. But she was light and he was dark. They walked the streets at night with their arms around one another and slept in an embrace despite the summer heat. They bought one another presents. He stroked perfume on to her skin and she trickled wine into his mouth. They exchanged edited accounts of their childhoods designed to amuse the other and to be generally illustrative of their shared belief in the shortcomings of New Zealand, which was a stern place, repudiating beauty unless in the form of scenery. An infantile land subject to sudden, unexpected furies. An unforgiving country where neither had ever felt at home.

These conclusions conveniently explained their departures. 'Although,' added Alexis, 'you don't notice that as a child. I was very happy.'

'Yes,' said Nerida. 'There was always food on the table. And the roads steamed after summer downpours.'

Mosquitoes bit your ankles after sunset.

The weather can be read from the west.

We ate the hearts out of nikau palms without thinking of the consequences.

We never turned our backs on the sea because we knew about the seventh wave.

The sea to the east is an odd milky turquoise colour we have not observed elsewhere anywhere in the world.

Our bare feet, conditioned by scoria, shells and boiling concrete, were impervious to injury.

Our fingers were lacerated by cutty grass.

Our calves were stained by paspalum.

The silence is alarming because there's such an onus on you to fill it.

It wasn't enough.

I was desolate. Kiss me.

Put your hand there and speak to me fantastically in your *belle-époque* voice, in your Las Vegas voice, in your Nazi voice, in all the voices I've wanted to hear that are in this reservoir, I think.

When Alexis woke one morning and refused breakfast, as he had warned her he would, Nerida was calm. She evacuated the house for the day so that he could play out his gripping, irresistible mood undisturbed. The weather was uncharacteristically sultry. Nerida strolled, instinctively, on the shady side of the street while English pedestrians crossed to the sunlit pavement. It interested Nerida that she still retained this protective habit that separated her from the English who had not grown up needing to avoid the excesses of the sun.

Alexis raged around the house, forcing himself to accomplish minor tasks – a telephone call to the bank, polishing his shoes, renewing a subscription. His head was heating up, its interior radiating electromagnetic energy. For a long time he gazed at the corkscrew hanging with other utensils on the kitchen wall. Longingly, he thought of trepanning. If there were a small hole in the side of his head, the beam of torturing energy could stream out of the vent.

While dodging aerobatic litter, which flew at low altitude down the funnel of Kentish Town Road, Nerida caught sight of a crowd of cameras, sitting in orderly rows in the window of a shop dealing in second-hand photographic equipment. Inside, she discovered a 16-millimetre camera, a superbly finished black-and-chrome, spring-driven Bolex H-16. When she put it to her eye she saw that it had a far-reaching depth of field. The camera balanced well in her hands, a simple yet substantial mechanism. She bought it for fun and returned to the roar of the street.

In the evening as Alexis lay sweating in bed, Nerida carried in a pitcher of iced water and kept him hydrated. After he had vomited in the bathroom she returned him to bed, wiped his face with a damp cloth, threw open the windows and placed her cool hand on his forehead. He stared at the elaborate, stuccoed ceiling. Horns blared in the street outside. Further in the distance, the swishing ebb and flow of traffic was as constant as waves on the sand.

'I should be at the beach,' Alexis said loudly.

'We'll go later,' Nerida replied. 'When it's not so hot.' Although there was no beach available in London.

His face was very pale and his hair was very black. He looked two-dimensional like a photograph. His fingers patted the sheet continuously. Nerida remembered sitting

93

at a bedside in the past. She would not abandon him. She knew the attack was only temporary, he had told her so. He would not abandon her. She did not know if he was aware of her presence or not but for her own sake, she lay down next to him.

Twenty minutes passed and then Alexis whispered, 'D'Alembert and Diderot and the encyclopaedia. A tree and a map and a maze.' Nerida dipped her hand in the cold water remaining in the pitcher and stroked his face. Alexis began to speak again, his voice flat and remote. 'D'Alembert said that the general system of the sciences and the arts is a kind of labyrinth, which the spirit faces without knowing too much about the path to be followed. But this disorder, however philosophical it is for the mind, would entirely degrade an encyclopaedic tree in which it would be represented. My head hurts.'

Nerida wrung a napkin in the water and pressed it over Alexis's forehead. It was wise not to speak. Not to act. She wanted to avoid trouble.

Alexis pushed the napkin away and stared at her blankly. 'He said our system of knowledge is made up of different branches, and I suppose most of them have a simple meeting place. But you can't simultaneously embark on all roads. The determination of the choice is up to each person's nature. It depends on the individual spirit.' Alexis closed his eyes.

Nerida woke at dawn to find herself alone. She crept to the study door, which was shut. Carefully she turned the handle and pushed the door open an inch. Alexis was at his desk, writing. He did not notice her. He remained there the whole day and most of the night. When he returned to bed, he slept for hours in a relaxed, splayed position in the fresh sheets, emptied of tension. At midday he wandered into the kitchen where Nerida was sprinkling chopped herbs into the soup simmering on the stove. Wrapping her in his arms he kissed the crown of her head. 'Alexis,' she sighed, 'I am so happy to see you again.'

'Do you have the patience to endure these cycles? It's very attractive, don't you think? All the throwing up and drenching of bed linen. Just as well you don't see me glaring bug-eyed at the wall in my study. That's when I'm really Mr Lunatic.'

'Why do you see a zed? Where does it come from?'

'I don't know. The swamp thing. Visual triggers are much more rare than aural or olfactory ones. But I don't ask questions about it.' He raised his hands above his head. 'I surrender, and there's a weird pleasure in that.'

'How do you feel now?'

His eyes gleamed. 'Ecstatic. Like I could leap over skyscrapers.'

Nerida laughed. 'I can live with that. I can live with you.'

Alexis placed his palms on either side of her head and pressed firmly. 'You're such a picture.' He licked her eyebrows. 'I'd like to eat you up, Nerida Simmonds.'

Taking her hand, he led her to the bed, where he consumed her mouth. For an hour they made love, and his return from the dead was sweet to her.

Later, while he was serving the soup, Nerida said, 'When my mother died, when I was seventeen, I felt responsible. I didn't realise how badly she was injured and I didn't phone the doctor. I was too busy thinking about myself.'

'But you were just a child. How could you recognise the seriousness?'

'That was no excuse.'

Alexis pulled her on to his knee, shaking his head. 'If there was an error, it was that you believed yourself to be powerful. A child has no power. Believe me, baby, I speak from experience.' He kissed her face so passionately, she slipped from his lap, dragging him with her. They collapsed on the floor.

'But the past no longer exists,' Alexis whispered. He covered her with his body. Alexis and Nerida sank into the anaesthesia of love. Sex. Love. Sex. Doubt and confusion deferred. The lover spears you with his gaze. The lover paralyses you with her touch. A fugue, in which life is reduced to one simple operation: submit to her power and presence, spread yourself at his feet. At this point you can do no wrong. You don't have to do anything because what you are is enough. You have found someone to save your life. A drug seeps through your veins and everything around you pauses while you drift . . . You've gone under, but you're in expert hands. She can slice your willing flesh. He can lay his hands on your pulsating heart. Nothing hurts. You happily fall on the knife.

13

Having encountered one another, it seemed for some time that Nerida and Alexis could be excused from enquiring into themselves. They believed that the happy convergence of their lives demonstrated the inescapable force of fate, which was a dangerous belief. Because the hand of fate is external and capricious. Sometimes it strikes a blow and sometimes it caresses, but its mission is always to seduce. Fate is a rake, a dominator, a dictator. You bend to its will and become helpless. You cease to find yourself convincing, although you probably never did, otherwise you would not so eagerly cherish the illusion that fate is capable of short-circuiting reality.

Nerida photographed compulsively, printing proof sheets for reference which she filed with the negatives in fat ring-binders, but her chief employment was self-education. She resolved to read every book in Alexis's library and he encouraged her. Without saying so, she believed that he could draw out her potential. This pedagogical exercise discharged fountains of sparkling conversation which inundated the pool of desire. Love and lack overlapped. Alexis and Nerida tumbled on to the bed or stood on the balcony at night, where he would lift her skirt, cupping her arse. She bit his lips. The breeze crept over her bare thighs as softly as a stalking cat. He penetrated her and she possessed him and when they came the temperature of the universe was 10,000° Kelvin – hotter than the surface of the sun.

It was on a mild Saturday morning, undistinguished by natural omens, that Drusilla's letter arrived. No blood moon, no croaking raven, no lightning-struck tree manifested in that particular area of Islington. But afterwards, an historian of human emotions might have identified this event as the psychological equivalent of assassinating the Archduke Ferdinand. The operations of ego, the reparations exacted for the crime of self-doubt, these constitute a world-wide empire.

The previous afternoon, a bomb warning had paralysed the West End. Alexis was incarcerated for two hours in a tube beneath Bond Street, leaving Nerida to entertain Francis Lipton, guest editor of the annual *British Anthropology Survey*. While salad leaves wilted and the sauvignon blanc reverted to room temperature, Professor Lipton made light of Alexis's absence. Nerida warmed to him. His sober bespoke suit was combined startlingly with an aged op-art tie, which instigated retinal confusion. His left ear-lobe was missing, as the result of a skin cancer, he volunteered cheerfully, contracted during field studies at Lake Disappointment in Western Australia.

With one eye on the darkening sky, he declared in a dozen different ways that Alexis's volume on Samuel Zeugen was eagerly anticipated. There was every reason to suppose it would be a landmark in linguistic thought. Alexis's forthcoming essay for the *Survey* could already be considered a harbinger of triumph. Finally, without venting the disquiet which Nerida knew must be percolating behind his complaisant, horsey face, Professor Lipton was forced to leave empty-handed and unfed. Although Alexis's delay was, on that evening, attributable to a chain of political decisions beyond his control, Nerida was aware that the essay, nevertheless, was overdue. She had seen it lying in fragments all over his desk. Despite Alexis's prodigious research, Samuel Zeugen stubbornly resisted capture.

In the morning Nerida found Alexis on his knees in the kitchen dismantling the waste-disposal unit. He gazed up at her. Pure and lovely Nerida. Her thin pale legs descending from beneath his white T-shirt. Her hair fluffed-up like a two-day-old baby chicken. She was lit incense. She was the stroke of a quill on a valuable vellum page. The sink was grimy with regurgitated coffee grounds and pulverised vegetable fibres.

'Blockage,' he said. 'I'm doing the masculine thing. Taking it apart.'

'Is it going to drive you crazy?'

'Yes. In about ten minutes I'll become unreasonably aggressive.'

'Then leave it.'

'Everything's in pieces.' He was holding a section of plastic pipe in the shape of a J. Then he dropped it on the smeared linoleum. 'You're right. I'll call an expert. Anyway, I only wanted a diversion. I'm supposed to be working.'

'Why don't you go back to bed? You look tired.' Nerida knew that, sometime before the end of the week, he would have a focal attack. And perhaps this time Zeugen would surrender.

Alexis rose from the floor and stretched his arms over his head, making himself into a looming elongation. 'I slept on the train yesterday. For the whole time we were stuck. I couldn't believe that two hours had gone by.' He glared at the disorder. 'I don't want to think about this. What a mess. Excuse me, *cara*,' he touched her shoulder, 'I'll have a drink.'

'It's eight o'clock.'

He frowned. 'Yes, you're right. I won't have a drink.'

A few minutes later Nerida heard him on the phone in the sitting room, raising his voice.

★　　★　　★

99

After buying a newspaper and a bunch of coriander, Nerida strolled in sunlight back to Dover Square. As she entered the square, she was struck by the beauty of the creamy, imposing Georgian houses, fused by architectural arithmetic into a unified aesthetic reckoning. Everything added up. Privilege equalled beauty. She and Alexis were from the same country but their backgrounds were oceans apart. This house was his home, inherited, without a struggle, from his parents. But for her, the house was an achievement, like her abundant bank accounts, which she would have never attained if she had not been, fortuitously, a pretty girl. This did not, she told herself, diminish her relationship with Alexis. Except that she sometimes wondered what might have happened if her existing intelligence, her thirst for knowledge, had been trapped in an unacceptable container. If her eyes were too small and her jaw too jutting and her body too lardy. If she had been compelled to wear clothes as a disguise instead of an enhancement. If she looked like the proverbial back of a bus. Wide and blunt and lumbering and no one could see past it. It was useful for transport but if you could, you'd take a taxi. Would anyone say then, 'Baby, baby, I adore your exquisite mind, your lambent, fucking lighthouse brain?'

An earthquake had ruptured the seabed. A tsunami had travelled with stealthy, deadly speed across the floor of the Pacific Ocean. On the front page of the newspaper, which Nerida was scanning as she walked, there was a picture of a coastal settlement in the Philippines being drowned by enormous, expulsive seas. She admired the technology that had permitted the destruction to be recorded. Reaching her house, she tucked the newspaper under her arm and shoved at the front door. It had warped in the recent rains. As she was precipitated into the hall, she saw that a thick airmail letter, addressed to Alexis, lay on the jute runner. There was no other mail, which was unusual.

They received daily a combination of packets and postcards along with bills, invitations to parties and Alexis's copious academic correspondence. The packets contained the many periodicals to which Alexis subscribed, while the postcards were generally addressed to Nerida – fleeting communications from models, photographers and associated fashion people far from home. Nerida had not yet recognised that she had no real friends. Apart from Alexis, she had never given herself to anyone. Already the postcards were becoming less frequent, because, believing herself to be absorbingly busy, she seldom replied to their senders.

Scooping up the letter, Nerida saw, her pulse quickening, that it was from D. Serafin, the fabled Drusilla. Her return address was Poste Restante, San Cristóbal de Las Casas, Chiapas, Mexico. Nerida had never met Alexis's older sister, who was a Red Cross doctor, married, he had quipped, to medicine, her rubber-gloved hands plunged deep in Third World gynaecology. Although he described their relationship as close, Alexis had not heard from her for two years – not even an acknowledgement of his letter announcing the existence of Nerida. Drusilla was always in an inaccessible place. Jabalpur or Bangui or Ujung Pandung. Nevertheless, she dwelt vibrantly in Alexis's thoughts. When we were growing up, he had related, she was unimpressed by the power of books and the prospect of university. She was a tourniquet of a girl, staunching the flow of our father, and so he left her alone. But she sneaked off down south to medical school, incidentally escaping the decline of our parents, and applied herself.

Slowly Nerida climbed the stairs, examining the spiky Italic handwriting on the envelope, pleased to be the bearer of glad tidings. Alexis would be delighted.

★   ★   ★

He smoothed the onionskin pages flat on the coffee table and read Drusilla's letter. He read it again. His pleasure in hearing from her was tempered by a slight disappointment. Although the envelope had felt substantial in his hand, he opened it to find that most of the weight came from the enclosed photograph, mounted on cardboard. There were only two and a half pages of actual writing, and a certain remoteness clung to them. Nerida observed a recessive smile on Alexis's face.

'What?'

He shook his head. The remoteness, of course, was deliberate. It was designed to make him want to know more which was Drusilla's way of verifying that their connection remained intact, despite the silence. He offered the photograph to Nerida. 'That's her.'

A hand-tinted woman stood enclosed by a border of doves and roses. Her high cheekbones, narrow dark eyes and black hair twisted into a single, heavy plait suggested tribal ancestry. Nerida could easily imagine an ancient version of Drusilla living vividly at an exotic address, probably a painted stone city deep in the jungle. Her appearance whispered: I hold the secrets of the tomb.

'You're very alike. Physically. She's beautiful. But you look more relaxed.'

'That's just my natural indolence.'

Drusilla had drawn many tiny arrows on the photograph, whose accompanying labels elucidated her items of clothing: indigo skirt, San Andrés Larrainzar, Chiapas. Ikat-dyed *rebozo*, Venustiano Carranza, Chiapas. Silk-embroidered *huipil*, San Juan Chileteca, Oaxaca. 3-metre woollen sash, San Juan Chamula, Chiapas. Alexis had told Nerida that, when Drusilla was not dealing with obstetrical events, she collected textiles.

'I'm curious about these meticulous labels.'

102

Alexis laughed. 'That's very Drusilla. She likes to pin things down.' He referred to the letter. 'She says, "As you can see, my journey through Oaxaca and Chiapas is sign-posted all over me. I don't appear in public like this, but in the privacy of my car I'm a shameless Mayan anthology. When I've discovered a new piece, I like to wear it immediately. (You know how I am.) The old pieces get preserved. I hope you're amused by the studio portrait. Here, everything is elaborate." She's writing because she may need to go to Paris soon. Which means she'll come here.'

Nerida returned the photograph to Alexis. 'To meet me?'

'Yes. To meet you.' Although Drusilla hadn't said that specifically. In fact she had made no mention at all of Nerida. Alexis took the letter to his study, from where he called, 'Do you feel like some fresh air? Let's go out. Get a sandwich or something and eat on the Heath.' He returned to the sitting room and pulled on his boots. 'Strangely enough, she's run into Eugene Rinehart. He's writing his book. The world is so minuscule. Why is that?'

Nerida closed and locked the french doors. 'Because it is composed of concealed symmetries which we desire terribly, otherwise the universe, and the future and various abstract nouns would be too big for us too handle.'

'Yes!' Alexis lifted Nerida off her feet and kissed her throat.

After a lengthy debate concerning freshness and authentic ingredients, Nerida and Alexis managed to buy slices of Spanish *frittata* from a young woman exercising gloom behind the counter of a delicatessen in Hampstead. They had to prove, in that English way, that they were worthy of service. During the truculent transaction, the shop had filled with customers, all of whom seemed to have pressing obligations elsewhere. A universal examination of wristwatches was accompanied by huffy, impatient sighs until, finally, the assistant thrust the slices into a bag and returned change to Alexis as if the coins were poisoned.

Once outside, Nerida and Alexis recovered their good spirits.

'England,' Alexis laughed, 'the world's most sado-masochistic country. I think that's why I don't live in America. Self-mortification is an art here and that regulates aggression. In America, you just pick up a gun.'

They walked on, negotiating the moving thickets of Saturday-morning shoppers whose need to gratify themselves with random, radical purchases was written on their pinched faces. Nerida appreciated this. The English were at their most emotional trying on a pair of gauntlets or agonising over a beaten tin mirror from a foreign country. While they were waiting for the lights to change, Alexis's gaze was forced towards a travel agent's window, where a laminated Z, an element of the words 'New Zealand', hung over a snow-capped mountain. Nerida, responding to the stillness of his body, turned to the window. At the sight of the magnificent peak, she experienced a retrospective spasm of loneliness. She stroked Alexis's sleeve, which felt warm and suggestive of woollen blankets on a freezing July night, when even the winterless north was penetrated by Antarctic southerlies.

'Would you ever go back?' she asked.

'Mmn. To do what? I don't know anyone there any more. After my mother died, everything dematerialised. It's an ominous phrase: "going back". It makes you think of revisiting some primal trauma. You don't want to go there, do you? It's alien.' Hooking his hand through the belt of her coat, Alexis directed Nerida over the zebra crossing. In the few minutes they had lingered at the intersection, the weather had altered. Fine rain began to fall, dampening their hair.

'I always wanted to find out that I was a holiday-making billionaire's mistake,' said Nerida, 'and he'd chosen to make up for his misdemeanours in a will that some fair-minded attorney found in a safety-deposit box in Honolulu. Leaving everything to me.'

The rain increased, slowly darkening all the surfaces around them. Alexis, because he was tall, had to dodge the sharp points of umbrellas which their fellow pedestrians were now wielding at his eye-level. 'We'll have to forget the Heath.' Running his fingers down the length of her spine, he said, 'Shall we go home?'

'I think we should do that.' Nerida threw the slices of *frittata* into a rubbish bin. 'We really fought for you,' she said as the bag subsided into the debris, 'but now we've changed our minds.'

Reaching the car, Alexis unlocked her door and then his own. As he started the engine, he saw that she had become quiet and locked-up.

'Are you unhappy?'

'No. I'm in love with you. I was thinking of the girl in the deli. That bad melancholy. It's like a recurring infection. Really hard to get rid of.'

'I won't let it happen to you.'

Their breath fogged the windows and Alexis had to drive by instinct until the humming demister melted the condensation. It left a nebulous residue so that Alexis thought that the expensive urban villages they drove through passed like scenes from a cinematic version (when ripple dissolves were all the rage) of a dream, or nervous breakdown. Drusilla said, the person who guesses how the Z connects, wins the game. She gazed sternly at her little brother. I'm afraid you didn't win. But she took pity on him. Baby, baby, kiss Mama. Then after a minute she added briskly, now you're grown up. It's time for the murdering game. Alexis raised his arm, clutching an imaginary dagger. With all his might he drove it at Drusilla but she was much stronger than he. Unyielding. He couldn't win that game either.

Alexis lay on his back on the Turkish rug in front of the fireplace. As Nerida bent to kiss him, she raised her arm. He clamped his hand around her wrist to hold her at bay. Nerida pressed down on him hard and Alexis withstood her, keeping her at a distance. Does that make you feel good? He said, yes. Do it again. She compelled; he resisted. It was a game in which they played out a fantastic erotic scene of excited forcings.

Eventually Nerida fell to one side, too weak to overcome Alexis. They lay in one another's arms, thinking separately. They had passed six months in a daze during which sexual passion concealed from them the turmoils and confusions that were incubating in their individual minds. Each feared, and it was an immense fear beyond conscious acknowledgement, that he or she was as vacuous as black, infinitely curved regions of space. That there was really nothing there to love; for who could cleave to a vacuum?

Nerida watched Alexis buttoning his shirt and then said, 'I admire your sister's work. She must be very dedicated.'

'She is.' He brushed at his jeans and stood up and reached out a hand to help Nerida to her feet. 'She was always sort of entire which made me envious. Even as a child she was already the theory of everything.'

'In other words, elusive.'

'Yes, exactly.' Alexis pulled on his jacket and kissed Nerida affectionately. 'I've got a few things to do. I'll bring back some wine.'

When he had left the house, Nerida walked about restlessly in the aftermath of intimacy, straightening cushions and stacking magazines, while her mind raced. You take a picture of a man smoking a cigarette. He is a television director. He has raised his arm to indicate that shooting will now take place. You take a picture of a dancer sewing up his bleeding foot. That's better. But secretly you would like to take other pictures. Yourself exposed, yourself as a victim of mood and circumstance and shivery coincidence which will not make its meaning clear. The dress you stabbed to death. The unanswered telephone. The word 'Sparta' you read just now in a book and the envelope, wrongly addressed to Mr G. Sparta, which has just fallen through the aperture in the front door. Pictures that say, Sadder Light of Love. How endless? Of what duration? Pictures of restraint: because emotions must be controlled to avoid craziness. Complicated restraint. Slippery hitch, stunner hitch, sheet or becket bend. The enigma of knots, bends, hitches, splices and seizings. A wedding at dawn. Afterwards the ritualists share a bottle of rum in the churchyard. Thin, smooth skin stretched over the pelvis, licked. The concentrated open mouth. Afterwards the ritualists share their secrets in a ruined bed. You would like to photograph examples of atmospheric perspective. And your lover's name painted red: example of vanishing perspective.

14

A man lay in bed thinking of his sister. Wherever she was, was home. Mrs Tcherne's baronial house was made of snow. No, Mrs Tcherne's baronial house was made of Oamaru stone. Like Mrs Tcherne herself, who had arrived on the same ship as the Serafins, speaking the same tongue. She had bought into local conditions. Alexis and Drusilla had been evacuated during the school holidays to this cold elegance while the domestic war raged at home. Snow fell on Southland as Drusilla ran across the far-reaching frozen lawn with a look on her face that said: Wait'll you hear this. Drusilla, mistress of weird correspondences, mistress of the twist. Sometimes she made Alexis laugh so hard he inadvertently began to cry, his chest heaving with emotion.

Once Drusilla and Alexis overheard a delivery boy singing in a language they could not understand. The song made Alexis feel sick with happiness. Drusilla was good at finding things. She delivered to him jokes and riddles, proverbs and shreds of rhyme that she scavenged from backyards and behind fairground stalls. Things that belonged to disadvantaged children. And she was alert to injury. She practised on him, wrapping him in splints and bandages.

He opened his eyes. He was in a strange bed in a strange house. Beneath an acreage of candlewick his body was restrained by a taut white sheet and a heavy blanket. His feet braced themselves hard against the footboard. Unclenching his right hand, which was stiff from cramp, he stroked the tufted parterres of candlewick, making a supreme effort to suppress his panic. Unmanly to cry out, to blunder from the bedclothes with a scenic display of hair-raking and hand-wringing.

Discreet birdchirp. Light flaring through pale holland blinds. Possibly late morning. A faint smell of mildew on the pillow together with a lack of personality in the bedroom – no dispersal of photographs, books or toiletries over the moody oak furniture – suggested that he was occupying a guestroom, although whose guestroom . . . a ten-foot-high question mark crouched over him. Any moment now a version of Father Bear would burst through the door. 'Somebody's been sleeping in my bed, and I'm going to punch his fucking head in.'

Shoving the covers aside, he confirmed with relief that he was fully clothed, his trousers still buttoned. No obvious evidence of depraved sexual activity or grave felonies committed. He slid his hand under the suave French wool of his jacket and found his wallet intact. Then a swelling hope propelled him from the bed. He was in a hotel. Or a bed and breakfast. It might just be possible to depart legitimately.

But when he raised one of the blinds, shutting his eyes at first against the attack of sunlight, he registered the depressingly suburban sight of high-walled gardens below. The gardens were attached to a barrier of terraced houses. A spasm turned him from the window. *Bathroom?* First need shoes. He swept the left one from under the bed but had to prowl the room for the other, stooping slightly from the tension in his groin. When he found the right shoe upside-down next to the dressing table, he wondered if he had kicked it off with great force the previous evening. Or previous week or month or year. Kicked off my shoes. Dived into a lacuna.

In the oval, tilted mirror of the dressing table he noted a dark beard already forming on his narrow face. Eyes bloodshot. Black hair collapsing over high forehead. The right side of his face ached, but there was no sign of injury, even though he felt as if someone had hit him hard. Passing a hand over his forehead, he saw that he had bony, rather soft hands. He had well-formed, clean fingernails. I wonder what I do for a living? Highly strung violinist? Something else with an L. Ling . . . ling, fish of the cod family, a kind of heather, lingo. Lingua franca. Lunatic. Look like a fucking lunatic. Unwashed appearance emphasised by the smell of stale sweat. Very nice. Reeking satyresque manifestation. Just lever cloven hooves into shoes and piss off. After bathroom.

Combing his hair back with his fingers, he let himself into a beige hall. He absorbed the silence of a family home vacated, he hoped, for the day. Work. School. Not knowing it harboured intruder. Zeugen found floating in deep harbour where white yachts sluice through green water. Bad pressure on his bladder.

He hurried on light feet to a door ajar at the end of the hall and achieved the nirvana of the lavatory. His urine, gallons of it, was the colour of Chablis. As he fastened his trousers in the postdiluvian stillness of the bathroom his mind was suddenly snagged by the memory of wine. Dinner party perhaps. Had he been here before as a guest of a colleague or the sister of an acquaintance? He started down the stairs of the meaningless house. Aiming for the front door, now only a few yards away, he realised that his hands were clenched, his breath trapped high in his chest. He was so tense that when, somewhere to his left, a motor started up a howling glissando, he cried out. He was answered by a scream.

Beneath an archway he saw a middle-aged woman connected to a roaring upright vacuum cleaner. Her eyes bulged and her head seemed to be bandaged with a terrible floral scarf. He started to laugh. Oh Dru, it was insane. Her eyes were bulging like she'd just recognised a strangler on duty and her head was bandaged with this terrible floral scarf. One of her arms was rigidly extended in order to feint at him with the vacuum cleaner. The hoover howled on as he sprang at the door, groped for the catch and released himself into the street.

Seeking a railway station and telephone he hurried along wide, empty pavements. The streets were so quiet he could hear the gnashing of leaves in the handsome trees. Name, name, come to me. In search of name, in search of Chablis. Then his smirking brain relented. Your name is Alexis Serafin. You wear scholarship as weightlessly and habitually as a silk shirt, although the one you have on at the moment badly needs laundering. You are a linguist. Remember? You have obligations. You have agreed to deadlines and your publishers are expecting you to bestow your customary free and easy brilliance on them. Not your insanity. Don't get the two confused.

Coming at last upon a strip of shops, he discovered that he was in Borehamwood on the brink of Hertfordshire.

Dr Alexis Serafin had always presented himself as a confident man. He had an attractive belief in his abilities which, when he was younger, envious academics had taken for presumption. He had never exhibited any fear of failure. Except that, if he thought of his childhood as a sentence, Papa, Mama and Drusilla formed the syntax, a structure larger than words; whereas he was the morph, the minimum visible or audible exponent of grammar. A man, in a moment of weakness, might think that he was put on this earth to replicate the high deeds of one parent and to earn the love of the other.

The train compartment was warm. He was alone in its cocoon listening drowsily to the glottal sound, the click and

111

clack, of train on track. No, not glottal. Click. He found his tongue retracting suddenly from his palate. They do that in Southern Africa, they click in their languages, the dental C, the retroflex Q, the lateral X, characteristic of (not like the pallid English example, *tsk tsk tsk*), characteristic of Zulu. Jesus, don't think Zulu, don't think Z. Close that window, *é pericoloso*. He let his head rest against the glass, while fields rushed by. He closed his eyes, immensely tired, having passed, it seemed, his one hundred and twentieth birthday. He had seen and lived everything. Now his hand was too frail even to pick up a book. Somebody read to me. The train said, *déjà vu, déjà vécu, déjà raconté, déjà éprouvé, déjà entendu . . .*

After Alexis had called her from Hertfordshire, Nerida had put down the telephone and, her legs shaking with the relief of hearing his voice, had sat down suddenly on the floor, breathing deeply. She felt weakened by the suspicion that a strong force was now about to intervene in her life with Alexis. This unnerved her. She did not like propulsion. She did not like cause and effect. She wished she could dip her hand into his brain and scoop out the offending part so that they would be tranquil and reprieved from chaos.

Hauling herself to her feet, Nerida fled into the refreshing, meditative bathroom, where hot flowing water was available, where a seclusion of mirrors welcomed unconditional self-admiration. After showering, she embarked on the ritual of make-up, smoothing her complexion and brightening her eyes and mouth, so that no trace of anxiety was visible. Make-up, it's a skill honed by women who conduct social interactions with the same tendencies, especially when their actions are enhanced by guilt: a smoothing and brightening takes place, a flurry of buffing and powdering so that everyone looks his – or her – best. But the subterfuges of women, Nerida thought, as she examined her newly immaculate self in the filmy mirror, were superficial and could be erased with a damp cloth or dispatched by the removal of their semiological clothes. Men, on the other hand, were both more clandestine and more anchored. Women embroidered the banners and arranged the flowers on the altar. Men were the doctrine. Except in cases where embroidering the banners constituted the doctrine and men had nothing to do because their mothers hadn't taught them the skills. Nerida sprayed a cloud of perfume into the air and walked into it, so that its musky fragrance permeated her, subtlely. She observed a tender, lovely woman standing in an expensively tiled bathroom, a woman who was aesthetically pleasing, and that impression generated calm. The telephone began to ring. Nerida flew to the receiver. It was Francis Lipton.

'Francis. How lovely to hear from you. Are you well?'

'I'm in fine form, Nerida. And you?'

'I'm very well. I must thank you for mentioning Margaret Mead to me. I'm reading her.'

'I'm delighted.' A dainty pause occurred. 'I wondered if I might speak to Alexis.'

'I'm awfully sorry, Francis. He's away – researching.'

Now the pause became more scrupulous. 'Ah.'

'May I give him a message? Actually I'm just about to meet him from the train.'

'It's nothing desperate. But I would rather like his copy.'

'Of course. I'll tell him.'

'Thank you so much.'

And then Nerida extemporised. 'He's suddenly discovered something interesting, I think, which he wants to include. Hence the delay. But he'll speak to you about it.'

'Wonderful! Please ask him to call me.'

'I will. Goodbye, Francis.'

With her doubts embalmed by this civil exchange, Nerida left for the station, where she would take Alexis in her arms.

Nothing was out of place. Nothing was broken. Except that degeneration is as startling as a crash.

Adopting the tone of a dinner party guest who is, over cognac, telling an amusing anecdote against himself for the entertainment of his companions, Alexis continued with his medical résumé. 'Then I began to experience a more intriguing pattern – sneaky ambulatory automatisms of which, at first, I had a small degree of awareness; but lately I haven't been able to recall these events at all. Two or three weeks ago, for example, we spent the weekend in Kent, with one of my editors actually, and his wife. While they were in the village, thank God, because I have no idea how I would have explained my embarrassing behaviour to them, Nerida discovered me on all fours in the herbaceous border digging a hole with my hands.' Alexis made his wry smile stretch a long way. 'Sometimes now I end up miles from home with no recollection of how I got there. Naturally, one is slightly alarmed.'

Alexis shot his cuffs, immediately irritated by the uncontrolled nervousness of the gesture, which was appreciated by Charles Stonehall, a neurologist of almost skeletal build, who sat behind the business side of a lustrous walnut desk in valuable consulting rooms off Cavendish Square. Stonehall scribbled an additional sentence on his notepad, then pointed his silver pen at Alexis. 'Do you still have seizures along the old order?'

'Yes. That's when I distill my reading, my research. But something strange is happening there, too. A few days ago while I was writing, I seemed to lose feeling in my fingers – '

'Are you right-handed?'

Alexis nodded. Instinctively he flexed his right hand, which at this moment felt perfectly normal. 'My brain, I thought, was unaffected. I kept on, despite the struggle to hold the pen, absolutely sure that I was writing clearly. However' – Alexis withdrew from the pocket of his jacket a sheet of paper which he unfolded and placed before Charles Stonehall – 'I'd like to know what you make of this. I was preparing a lecture on functional linguistics.'

Lowering his head, Stonehall squinted at the paragraph. Alexis wondered if Stonehall needed glasses, though it seemed odd that a medical man would not correct so mundane a fault. Unless, of course, it was a question of vanity. As the neurologist frowned over his patient's slanted handwriting, with its deep, swooping descenders, Alexis mentally reread the offending words, which were written inerasably on the blackboard of his mind: 'The degree to which Saussure inspired the initial theories of the Prague Group is a source of some debate. His student, Sergej Karcevskij, along with Trubetzkoj and Jakobson, was one of the three signatories of the remarkable proposition presented to the first congress of linguists at the Hague in 1928. In the first language is producing of human actionivity which ha a caractere finalsim direct feelingness but Saussure raise barrier against discover strucfgyuul laws of linguini systems which compared need to be genetically rererelated.'

'Obviously I can't continue like this.' Alexis laughed.

After a pause, Stonehall said, 'Well, judging by the jumble we have here, there's definitely a spot of bother in the left lobe. I think we might want to run a few routine tests.'

'Such as?'

'An EEG analysis. A brain scan. And we'd take a little sample of the cerebro-spinal fluid.' Glancing up from beneath tufty eyebrows, he directed a professionally reassuring smile at Alexis. It looked, however, like the smirk of an executioner. Alexis breathed deeply in order to quell the racing of his heart. Stonehall could not help his saturnine appearance, his hair-covered hands and beetle-brow.

'I suppose,' Alexis shrugged, 'there's the possibility of a tumour or something equally sinister.'

'There's always that possibility, but let's not go mad thinking of worst cases. We'll wait for the results of the scan.'

'I'd like to think it's simply a psychomotor epilepsy.'

'My dear chap, there's no such thing as a simple psychomotor epilepsy.'

'But it can be treated with medication?'

'In many cases, yes, an anti-convulsive will curb focal attacks. In fact I'm surprised you've managed for so long without treatment.'

'I did not see the need. The seizures have a sort of order to them and anyway, they have enhanced my work.'

'Up until now. You might, you know, benefit far more conclusively from a surgical intervention.' Stonehall said this languidly, as if the idea were of little consequence. 'It's early days yet of course but I'd like you to know that the option exists.'

Instantly a bolt of protest charged through Alexis at the idea of surgery. Alexis's wordless negative response, Stonehall went on, smoothly, 'Given that you presented with meningitis as a child, the scan is likely to show some cortical scarring. Then we'd whip out the bad stuff. Sixty to eighty per cent of epileptics who opt for surgery are completely cured.'

'What are the drawbacks?'

Stonehall held up his pencil-thin index fingers in close opposition, as if he were demonstrating a very small measurement, while at the same time, his words communicated to Alexis an insurmountable gulf. 'There could be a subtle impairment of short-term memory. Sometimes the language function is affected.'

116

Rising from the enclosure of his art deco armchair, Alexis gazed at the numerous water-colours, all executed by the same hand, which hung on the hessian-covered walls. He shook his head. 'I couldn't take that risk for a moment. I'm a writer – a linguist. A linguist with a language dysfunction, that's like handicapping a runner with orthopaedic footwear.'

'On the other hand, Dr Serafin,' Stonehall countered, attaching a delicately ironic nuance to the title of 'Doctor', 'a linguist with temporal lobe problems is an equally unreliable prospect.'

The paintings were pastel abstracts, whose water-colours had dribbled everywhere, soaking into the once wet paper. Seeing that Alexis was captivated by these works of art, Stonehall waved a deprecating hand while also squaring his narrow shoulders, and admitted, 'I'm afraid I'm the culprit. It was a toss-up between the scalpel and the easel when I was young. I still like to keep my hand in. It relaxes one.'

'I couldn't agree more,' Alexis replied with automatic politeness and then realised a second later that he couldn't agree less. He had once believed that the achievement of anything should be conducted with a dissembling casualness, but it struck him now that the exercise of art, whatever form it took, required tension as tight as a death-provoking ligature. The relaxation, the relief, came afterwards when you were liberated from its torment and discovered that something eucharistic had taken place, although Alexis realised that he, personally, had not transmuted his compulsions into anything that served as a detour, no matter how meta-phorical, around mortality. Nor, evidently, had Charles Stonehall, but this observation suddenly increased Alexis's confidence in the neurologist. Stonehall's expertise with stainless-steel instruments, with electrodes and infra-red monitors, must surely surpass his indecisive manipulation of the sable brush. A sensible man, a successful man, pursues the path of obvious talent, not the path of wishful thinking.

'Of course I'll do the tests. It would be foolish not to.' Alexis returned to his chair, arranging his limbs to illustrate composure. 'But my preference is for medication. I won't submit to surgery, I can't.'

Stonehall acknowledged this with a slight bow of the head. 'Depending on what we find, we can try a course of carbamazepine for six, twelve, months. It doesn't suit everyone and there's only about a forty per cent chance of complete freedom from attacks, but we must hope for the best. The side-effects vary. Some people feel intoxicated by it. Others suffer from fatigue or depression. But that would be preferable to the deterioration you are experiencing now.'

'Yes, it would.' Optimism burst into the room like a devoted dog that had accidentally been locked outside, and was now throwing itself at the feet of its master. Who was in charge and in control. Alexis was convinced that he could overcome the affliction of his wayward brain and he hoped that he'd never have anything to do with medicine and madness again. He lounged in his artefact of a chair while Charles Stonehall wrote a letter of clarification. Outside, mid-morning sunlight burnt off the hard frost that had covered the streets of London with a beautiful caul.

15

Touch me. That urgent invitation had followed on from, would you like some tea? And was accompanied, under the quilt, by an instinctive commentary: Do you believe in the magnificence of symbolism? Was Don Giovanni *really* threatened by a chorus of underground demons? What did you do today? Did Newton's breakdown compromise his thinking so that modern physics is allayed to a death-oriented view of nature? After you left I buried my face in your shirt. Will the Government collapse? Would life be easier if you surrendered all your books and musical and scientific instruments in order to live in a cell, bare except for some small books of devotions and a few hair shirts and scourges? Why is it, despite the passing of time, that I can't stop kissing your shoulders?

People such as Nerida and Alexis, who might have been accused, by inert human beings with the sensibility of a darning egg, of thinking too much, could not help themselves. During childhood they had conformed to the instructions of their mentors, who took various forms – teacher, parent, stockman, sister – but fundamentally intimated that the absorption of texts, including TV, magazines, street signs and billboards, would fully round them into adults who understood the purpose of their existence on this watery, oxygenated planet. In fact, Nerida and Alexis were so expectant, mouths gaping in anticipation like fledglings in the nest, of a three hundred and sixty degrees' experience of life lived, that they flung themselves at pornography and philosophy with indiscriminate abandon which meant that they were isolated. They possessed radio-active auras that repelled relatives, colleagues, neighbours and acquaintances. They suffered from romance and were wary of elitism. Their states of mind were compatible with the atmosphere of legend. They couldn't help, individually, wondering about Psyche and Eros or Narcissus and Echo or any other quasi-historical couple programmed for actions which would draw the attention, later, of scribes dressed in metres of wild linen, who had nothing better to do but hang about in the agora writing down big-time gossip – later it would be validated by psychological premises. Love is written of and sung about and agonised over, universally and synchronistically, because it is a lot less common than is advertised.

It's mythological. It's disconcerting and obscure. It is not a mean ambition to be in love, even though it has been debased by television mini-series and sexual politics. Anyone can become, with proper encouragement and training, a veterinarian, a surveyor, a drain-layer, a wig-maker, an estate agent, an electronics engineer, a screen-printer, a chef, a school principal, a professional badminton player, a florist, a barman, a district nurse. But few people are accomplished lovers, since they need to be both desperate and self-assured as well as being disciples of paradox; practitioners of simultaneous submissions and dominations. This definition excludes dumb abusers who act purely from lonely, neurotic motivations. It is the ecstatic element that is so evanescent. That expectation derives from reading and its off-shoot, the screen industry. That was the conditioning of Nerida and Alexis who were doomed to be exceptional. That was hard.

Twisting the cord, Nerida laughed into the telephone.

Alexis was saying, 'And then there's this very demented

one with a French accent as thick as platform plimsolls. He's delivering a paper on trivial metaphors. I miss you, *cara*. I love you.'

'Which is my pleasure. Who else is there?'

'Well, as usual there's a yawning absence of women. Just a clutch of arrogant boy-professors, whatever their ages, being rude to the servants. Bring me my drinking horn, wench. I have an over-developed brain. I am Zormax, the Mighty Noun, waster of empires!'

'Or possibly, members of a now abandoned division of invertebrates.'

'Yes! I have to go in a minute. I hear the blare of trumpets. Wusniak is due to speak on the hieroglyphic sign.'

'That sounds hot.'

'Girls are screaming in the streets.' Alexis sighed. 'I've got to get out of this pouty mood, Nerida. I've written a good paper, but my attitude's bad. My mind should be a ballroom with all the chandeliers blazing.'

'So, flick the switch.'

'I'll try. Listen, I'll be home around seven. Are you going out?'

'I've already been out.' She had attended a screening of three short films, *Oh Dem Watermelons* and *Hold Me While I'm Naked*, followed by a piece existing of one continuous shot, in which a pair of hands, a man's, patiently unravelled a knotted fishing line. Over a period of fourteen minutes the line was unthreaded and unlooped and untangled with pliant, logical finesse until the last complication of the awful backlash was dispatched and the line once again, describing a simple arc in the air, could resume its function. Nerida had been captivated by the dissolution of the backlash. This image had filled her heart with hope, while her mind had leapt at the unadorned expression of an idea. She would tell Alexis about it later in return for an exposition of his

121

day. 'I'll spend the afternoon taking some pictures or maybe reading.'

'Watch that. It's a bad habit. It'll turn your head.'

'OK, I'm going. Alexis, how do you feel?'

'Like a new man. I wonder if anyone will notice a difference.'

'Not your·illustrious peers . . . too deep in the linguistic substrata to read people.'

'I don't know. There's a lot of talk about psychoanalysis at this conference. Most of it comes from experts with unhappy lovers and disturbed children, or no lovers and no children, since I doubt whether anyone here has ever experienced a carnal event. Jesus, I'm acid today. I sound like my father.'

'Don't throw it in their faces.'

'No. I won't disfigure anyone. I'd prefer a nice, clean kill.'

'Then stay calm.'

'Yes, ma'am. On approaching the podium I'll slip into my biathlete disguise – heartbeat rapidly reduced despite the exertion of skiing at speed across the quadrangle, my rifle raised with rocksteady aim.'

'And then you'll pick them off one by one. Wusniak. Murchison. Even Francis.'

'Francis has already been mortally wounded by my failure to contribute to his *Survey*. I owe him.'

'You should have told him why.'

'No.'

There was a silence. Nerida could not even detect the sound of his breathing. 'Alexis?'

'I must go. I'll see you tonight.' He hung up before Nerida could say anything else.

She unlocked the french windows and opened her box of tricks. Both she and Alexis liked air to circulate through their house. They slept with the window ajar. In the sculptured

122

polystyrene interior of the aluminium case, lenses were buried, along with a light meter and two Nikon camera bodies. Nerida had insisted that Alexis see Charles Stonehall, and it was unclear whether he would hold it against her. Sometimes she suspected that he was keen to blame someone. But it did not seem right to her that a person's sense of himself should depend on a sickness, even if that sickness did masquerade as brilliance. It had been difficult for her to assert an opinion. That was at odds with her desire to be a gorgeous, chiffon-trailing integer who filled their house with bunches of emphatic flowers, even in winter. She paid the maximum price for hothouse blooms imported from Holland.

The scan had not disclosed the ghostly whiteness that indicated the presence of a tumour. No operation was required. Alexis had responded decisively to the prescription of carbamazepine, which completely suppressed his focal attacks. True, he sometimes behaved like a man intoxicated, but his raddled actions – we are flying now to the Lenox for twenty-four hours in memory of slow tides of delight; I won't eat in a building that looks like an aircraft carrier; what was I saying? I keep falling asleep – had ebbed as the weeks passed. He was fine. After monitoring his condition for three months, Stonehall was persuaded (if not satisfied; he would have preferred an observation period of six months but Alexis convinced him otherwise) that his patient had stabilised. High in the heavens, Nerida and Alexis circled in a holding pattern, expecting permission to be granted imminently to descend into everydayness. Unknown to them both, Drusilla was flying at 35,000 feet over the arctic on her way to London.

Alexis left the common room and hurried along a glassed-in corridor towards the auditorium. Hailstones clattered against the glass, but this localised meteorological drama did not divert anyone. Impossibly young students, thundering over the industrial carpet, were concerned only with library fines, skin problems and sexual anticipations. They did not own any of the cars, parked in the street below, whose panels were being subtly indented. It was possible to move around the campus, by way of underground tunnels and covered bridges, without encountering the elements. Undeniably, Alexis told himself, as he emerged on to the stage of the lecture hall by way of a staff entrance, his release from the trance-world had suffused him with a sense of freedom. Yet his dreams were filled with doubt.

I tried the door to a familiar room. The door was difficult to open but I forced it. It's always difficult, even though I have a key. But once inside, I could write with my hands tied behind my back. Nothing to it. Now I walked in so easily, simply glided through walls; the room wasn't even there. A trace memory made me rush about, searching. I thought I detected structure but the chair and the desk had vanished. With my finger, I drew a Z on the wall. But it was lifeless. There was no aura, no field of energy. No psychic tremble. Just a mark in the dust which looked like an act of petty vandalism. I was bereft. I could hear the shuffle of normal people outside in the street, walking up and down, normally.

Attaching a long lens to her camera, Nerida stepped on to the balcony. Above, stratified clouds were in the process of being mutated by pollution. Below, crawling cars forced themselves into the sclerotic arteries leading from the square. From her elevated position, Nerida considered London. During the miracle play entitled *Alexis's Illness*, it had become unreal, its concrete details – architecture, roads and restaurants and belching buses – dissolving into a monumental background wash which served as a neutral ground for the theatricals downstage. She had reduced her interactions with the city and its society to practically nothing. Context had faded from her life. She was engaged in a struggle with a larger frame of reference. I guess! she said to herself. What's your problem? The idea of being an astronaut was attractive. The idea of careless floating, released from gravity into the unframed, limitless arena, occupied by small scientific tasks, small maintenances, whose significance would be decided by others.

Bracing herself against the iron railing, she raised her camera. In the middle of the square, a couple was circling around one another, like lyre birds; he was raising his arms so that his overcoat flapped, increasing his bulk, and she was shaking a head of long ringlets which shivered and tossed in a display of feminine attraction. Nerida scrutinised them through the lens – they were talking, gesticulating – and then began to photograph them. The couple became still, glaring at the ground. The woman bent to fasten her shoe. Her lover thrust his hands into her hair and then pressed her face to his thighs. She ascended into his embrace and they kissed, swaying with the force of emotion. Nerida thought to herself: It's not true as physicists say, wrecking their lives to prove it, that one and one do not necessarily make two. It gave her great satisfaction to sequester this unknown woman and man on film, their image reversed. Because when she printed the picture, if she ever did, there would be a further reversal and the recovery of the image's inverse symmetry.

Nerida's camera followed the couple as they strolled loomingly towards her. But as they reached the pavement, they were effaced by a black taxi which halted in the street opposite the house, filling the snug frame hugely. Nerida lowered her camera. A small woman dressed entirely in red emerged from the cab. As she surveyed the house, the sinking sun illuminated the strong planes of her face. Catching sight of Nerida on the balcony, she raised a hand in greeting, as if they were old friends. The taxi drove away. Nerida returned the wave, feeling a frisson of apprehension, for surely this was the superior Drusilla.

Holding her drink, Drusilla stood by the fireplace like a man, with her elbow resting on the mantelpiece, while Nerida sat at a lower level on the sofa, riveted. Drusilla's dramatic clothes and striking looks invoked an emblem – a symbolic device, an inlaid ornament – standing for strength of character and fixity of purpose, of a woman who took people in hand.

As Drusilla spoke effortlessly and amusingly about her travels, accompanied by articulate gestures and challenging eye-contact, Nerida concluded that Alexis's sister was extremely accomplished at *mise-en-scène*. She understood the importance of the whole picture, of the eloquence of presentation. Employing an amiable and reassuring doctor's manner, she asked questions about Nerida's life, which Nerida automatically evaded in order to forestall judgement. Drusilla seemed more than capable of making a dispassionately devastating diagnosis, but, like any patient, Nerida did not wish to know the worst. At the same time, she was impressed by Drusilla's interrogatory technique. Her conversation with Alexis's sister made her think about the people she knew – friends, or at least acquaintances. They very rarely enquired, with conviction: How are you? I am seeing you, not in order to speak infinitely about myself, but to engage in an equal exchange of feelings and observations. Most people Nerida knew used their friends as sounding boards only. You could say the most extravagant thing – I sent away for a suicide kit which arrived yesterday morning and I've already ground up the halcion for use around midnight in conjunction with 500 mls of gin – and this friend would interject, did I ever tell you about the time that *I* tried to commit suicide . . .? Drusilla, on the other hand, divulged nothing about herself.

'This,' she said, 'is a rather beautiful piece of technology.'

126

She had strolled over to a drop-leaf table on which was lying Nerida's Bolex camera. 'It must be yours. I don't remember Alexis being very visual.'

'Yes, it's mine. The controls are crowded but it's easy to use. It's fantastically basic, but I like it for that reason. It requires enthusiasm. It's like driving a manual-shift car. You could afford an automatic but you just like the feeling of manipulation, the hand-eye co-ordination.'

'You must show me one of your films then.'

'Actually, I haven't made any. I'm low on ideas.'

'Really? That must be a dilemma.' Drusilla returned to her position at the mantelpiece.

Nerida said, 'Alexis will be thrilled to see you.'

Drusilla asked, 'And how is he? How is his state of mind? Poor baby.'

Nerida inwardly bristled at the 'poor baby'. It suggested an unfair diminishment of Alexis, and moreover, if she was in the mood to be paranoid, an assumption by Drusilla that Alexis was not happy, which was untrue. He and Nerida were wildly in love, although it was not possible to state that openly without sounding like an adolescent. Something about the presence of Drusilla forbade such a declaration. Nerida wondered what deceptive situations had taken place in Alexis's childhood. She volunteered nothing about his epileptic turbulence, preferring to conceal this fact so that she had something over Drusilla, without understanding why she should feel motivated to engineer such a petty triumph.

'Alexis is fine. He's brilliant.'

'As ever. And what is he speaking on in Sussex?'

'Dictionaries.'

'Oh no,' Drusilla laughed. 'When will he move on?'

'Your father, I believe, trained him up.'

'So you've heard about Papa? Of course you have. Intimate relationships invite discussion of parents, don't they?'

127

No! Nerida wanted to insist. Intimate relationships invite transcendental sex. They invite crazy primal statements. They invite terrible exposure that depends on trust. But it was important to like Drusilla, since she and Alexis were so close, at least historically. Suppressing her agitation, Nerida refilled Drusilla's glass.

'Thank you. It's nice to drink wine. Mexico's a country of beer.'

Nerida relaxed again and smeared caviare on a cracker, which Drusilla refused.

'They drove me mad, those dictionaries. Honestly!' Abandoning her glass on the mantelpiece, Drusilla plumped herself on the sofa next to Nerida and gazed into her eyes so that Nerida was once more charmed by Drusilla's close attention. 'As far as I was concerned, all those dictionaries were just a collection of restricted inventories. They supply you with semantic knowledge, but they don't come with instructions for use. Dictionaries are language at its most primitive. They are useless.'

'Then no doubt you and Alexis have had many lively discussions on that point. Linguistics is his life.'

'I don't think so.'

'How can you know? You haven't seen him for years.'

'That doesn't matter. I know him.' Drusilla leaned back into the sofa and looked piercingly at Nerida, apparently to remind the bride that there were many things she did not understand; that she was not privy to the complete story. In this moment Nerida disliked Drusilla for her privileged position as the sister. She also liked her for her intransigent beauty, and the power she exerted. And she was frustrated by the see-saw of emotions that Drusilla had generated in the space of one hour and ten minutes. Drusilla, Nerida understood, expertly manufactured ambivalence. She withheld things – she gave the impression that she guarded great valuables – and that

128

caused you to propitiate her, hoping to receive, while at the same time resenting her mandate.

'I hope you and Alexis can survive together,' Drusilla stated, suddenly.

Nerida was taken aback. 'What makes you say that? We are perfectly happy. We talk. He's an amazing person.'

'I know.' Then she added, 'I suppose you are fortunate.'

'Sometimes it's hard work. Sometimes it's painful.'

'Exactly.' Drusilla uttered this word with the reverberance of a castle gate being bolted against a siege.

The front door slammed, which was followed by the percussion of Alexis's footsteps and then the living-room door was pushed open. Alexis shoved his hair back from his face and enacted a slow-motion sequence of opening his mouth and dropping his briefcase.

'Dru!' Alexis held out his arms. Drusilla jumped to her feet and clasped her hands in front of her chest, smiling. Alexis glanced at Nerida with widened eyes, but he ran to Drusilla and embraced her, hard. These are siblings of one another, Nerida thought, tightly related by a principle that says they are the same thing. Alexis looked suddenly like a small boy, even though he was much taller than his sister. He inclined his body during their embrace, as if he wished to reduce his size. Nerida saw in this moment that it could take a very long time to know someone, especially when he had more than one personality.

Over a dinner of Indian takeaways which Nerida had ordered while Alexis and Drusilla engaged in hilarity, Drusilla revealed the reason for her visit. She had a ravaged Constantin sedated in a hotel room in Marylebone. His alcoholism had finally flooded his life, drowning everything. This intelligence caused a change of temperature at the dining table. The light in Alexis's eyes flickered and grew dim momentarily before his concern for Constantin established itself. He laid down his fork and sitting back in his chair, asked of Drusilla, 'How did you know?' Nerida identified a faint accusation in his voice.

'We've always kept in touch. A month ago he wrote to me.'

'That's a tribute to your charismatic personality. Constantin's not the letter-writing type. Are you sure Linda didn't dictate it?'

'Not unless she was incoherent at the time. I phoned him. He could hardly speak. He'd disintegrated.'

'He could have contacted me.'

'I think he was ashamed. Men don't call on one another in that way. They always look for the hand of a woman. Don't you agree?' Drusilla smiled at Nerida, a trenchant smile which Nerida interpreted as judgemental; Drusilla the officer assessing the capabilities of Nerida the new recruit.

'But he has a wife,' said Nerida. 'Alexis has described her as a paragon of practicality. Why isn't she taking care of him?'

'Because Constantin's collapse terrifies her. It's the collapse of his psyche and that is something Linda cannot fix up. She's helpless in the face of it.'

'What can I do?' asked Alexis.

'I've found a clinic near Bath. They'll dry him out. It's a good place. Expensive.'

'Who's paying?'

'Linda. She would like him to be well, to be restored to her.'

'Is that possible?' Alexis asked.

Drusilla gazed at him without speaking, then she tore a strip off a chapati and mopped up the remains of the dhal on Alexis's plate. 'You know how I hate waste.' She chewed the food delicately, then licked her fingers. 'The thing is, it will be a few weeks before they can take Constantin.' Turning to Nerida, Drusilla placed her warm hand on Nerida's arm.

'I know this is an extreme request, but could he stay here until then?'

In the amniotic darkness of their bedroom, Nerida lay with her cheek pressed against Alexis's smooth shoulder-blade, her body curved around his buttocks and thighs. His limbs were heavy with fatigue, but he was restless. Twisting on to his back, he let an arm fall diagonally across her, keeping her close.

He murmured into the night, 'You don't mind having Constantin here? You don't have to agree to it.'

'I don't mind. It would be unjust to abandon him.'

'Yes.' Alexis rearranged his pillow and folded his hands beneath his head. 'Drusilla always asks for a lot.'

'Constantin's important to her.'

Alexis pushed the duvet away. 'I don't know what happened between them, if anything. I once gave Drusilla Constantin's address years ago when she was going to Paris for a course. I was in America at the time. Drusilla and I never seemed to coincide in our travels. They spent time together. More than you would expect. You'd think that Drusilla would have found his unreliability unacceptable. But women like Constantin. They seem to believe that he will dominate them, although the opposite is true.'

'That's what attracts them.'

'When I was a child, I relied on Drusilla as if she were a parent. I think my actual parents were frightened of her. She saw right through them. She thought they were weak. I only realise now how much I wanted to please them. But she never seemed to have the same compunction. I need to sleep. If I keep talking I'll start to dream and I don't want that. Put your hand over my face. I can breathe through your fingers.'

They fell asleep. Near dawn Nerida woke and groggily made her way to the bathroom. As she returned to the bed,

Alexis seized her and buried his face in her groin. His tongue licked at her and his fingers brushed over her nipples, which swelled and hardened. He hauled himself up so that he was suspended over her. The tip of his cock sought the space between her legs. Their tongues tangled and slipped around one another and he entered her. But he could not stay erect. He pushed himself at her unsuccessfully. Why can't I do this? I want to. Use your fingers, she whispered. Use your mouth. After her body had ceased shuddering, he sat up with his back against the bedhead and dragged her across his lap. She felt limp, her mind emptied.

Alexis hung on to Nerida. He gripped her hair. He said, when she uttered his name, don't speak. And when she attempted to adjust her position, because he was leaning heavily on her, he said, don't move. Please stay exactly like this.

Drusilla comes and she goes. She cares only for herself. Or for someone other than me. She's an involution, a complicated grammatical construction, graceful and symmetrical and turned in on itself. She's a formidable and beautiful caryatid holding up the pediment of the temple, where I have worshipped. Over the centuries the features of her face have become obliterated by wind and rain, but she remains integral. She has not crumbled. There's a rope around the temple now so that tourists cannot enter and cause damage to the monument. It is more fragile than it looks. Now you can only admire it at a distance.

16

Constantin's luggage consisted of a single black rubbish bag bulging with books whose angles had perforated the plastic. He arrived in a daze, accompanied by Drusilla, who had supervised his transference from Paris. Refusing, mutely, to give up his belongings to Alexis, Constantin clomped up the stairs, dragging the disintegrating sack behind him. He had barely reached the spare bedroom, to which Alexis cheerfully directed him, when the polythene shredded completely, disgorging unwashed clothing on to the floor, along with the books and a large quantity of metro tickets. Unconcerned, Constantin fell on to the bed and sank straight away into a profound, snoring sleep.

Drusilla stayed no more than an hour, which period of time she packed tightly with so many efficient administrative details concerning the sanitorium in Somerset, and clinical observations about alcoholism, and a description of the obstetrical practices of Michel Odent at Pitiviers where she was due the next day to observe a water-birth, that Nerida and Alexis were prevented from squeezing in the slightest query about her state of mind. Deftly, she buckled down and closed the conversation. Then, quickly consulting her watch, Drusilla darted to the door, where the three of them engaged in civil kisses and embraces and made a non-specific arrangement to meet in the near, virtual, future. Both Alexis and Nerida were conscious of Drusilla's almost painful need to avoid anything emotional. It overrode Alexis's desire to ask, when will we meet again, exactly? They let her escape into the street, where she immediately commanded a taxi to stop and was gone, leaving the havoc of Constantin behind.

'That was strange,' Nerida said, shutting the door.

'I'm used to it,' Alexis replied.

When Alexis was away from the house, Nerida remained with their somnolent guest, who passed a week slumped on his bed. Eventually Nerida persuaded Constantin to stand, and then to leave the bedroom. He put his sweater on back to front. He couldn't shave without damaging his face. He vomited on the dining table. Alexis apologised and cleaned up the mess, but Nerida was not disquieted. Constantin was her patient and she was prepared to do anything to repair his condition. She was not disturbed when anger kidnapped his fundamentally sweet self. Shouting in the night; storming into the dining room, raving about the Moscow School. But after a couple of weeks, he improved, becoming docile. Nerida agreed that he could have one bottle of wine a day if he would eat the meals she cooked.

For six weeks Constantin worked day and night in his room. Alexis supplied him with books and stationery. It astonished Nerida that Constantin still retained some island in his distressed brain where thought was fecund and paradisal and effective. Alexis, standing unnoticed at Constantin's bedroom door, envied that extraordinary, extra-material concentration, that motiveless drive. Alexis, who was contracted to deliver four lectures to – to – the institution escaped him, felt hackneyed. Trite and ordinary. He turned from the door, in search of the benefits of sanity.

Constantin was silent on the nature of his studies. Instead, he would emerge around seven in the evening, demanding that Nerida describe the minutiae of her day. I don't know how to cook, Nerida. How did you make this food come out like this? And your car, what colour is the upholstery? Is everything in acceptable working order? The interior light? You can wind down all the windows? I don't know how to drive. You put the key in the ignition. Then what happens? How do you make the car go?

Then Constantin stopped speaking. Once more he forgot to put on his shoes. He clung to a pillow, unable to find his way out of the bedroom. Fortunately, at this point a vacancy arose in Somerset. Nerida and Alexis drove him to the clinic which was disguised as a manor house. Nerida brushed Constantin's hair and whispered, I've just realised that too many women have done this for you, but he remained uncognizant. They spoke to Linda on the telephone. I will pay anything, she said, just to have him back. How long will it take? Will they fix him up? I don't understand.

Nerida fetched up in Knightsbridge, obeying an imperative of her dream universe: euphoria is connected to the wearing of good clothes and a tactile lavishing of love on yourself which is a displacement for . . . cleverness! Empathy! Nerve-tingling recognition of specialness. When you were a girl in red-clay, hard-sky New Zealand foraging for a manifestation of this, although you didn't realise it at the time, what would have been the furthest thing from Northland, from stalagmited-and-tited caves, and secretive deep harbours, whose existence was only considered existent when recorded by foreign experts? The furthest thing was a discriminating department store specialising in gratification. Nerida tried on clothes, which she was not interested in buying, but the sharp-eyed assistants cosseted her, believing her to be *echt*. Pukka. The genuine article. And Nerida thought: How ridiculous. This no longer works. I'll have to give up being a sub-clause of style.

She had just watched a three-hour-long piece of animation weirdness called *Heaven and Earth Magic*. It had trickled, over a period of twenty years, out of the brain of the famously peculiar Harry Smith. A film which made feverish, irrational enquiries of the occult and the neurophysiological. Salamanders, sarcophagi and skeletons lurched across the screen. The heroine sat in a dentist's chair and was given an anaesthetic. She ascended to heaven in search of a watermelon stolen by a dog. Harry Smith made a terrifyingly mutable world by cutting out and pasting pieces of paper. The heroine had been scissored out of an old shopping catalogue. This painstaking task had consumed much of Harry Smith's life on earth. Nerida drove back to Islington, with a vocation dancing just out of reach, thinking about the drugged heroine who returned to this planet even after being eaten by the head of an old philologist; thinking about obsessive mentalities.

While Nerida was trapped in traffic, Alexis sat at his desk, ignoring the blinking light of the answerphone. There were a number of messages. All basically saying: What next? When will you? Why the silence? Deadline! He was not working at all. He wrote carefreely to Eugene Rinehart, thinking: Why not? There might be a payoff there. And he wrote to Drusilla who had returned to Mexico. And he fixed himself a gin and tonic and turned on the TV and said to himself, look I'm simply being recreational. It's permitted. People everywhere watch television and eat takeaway Chinese and do not agonise about the cauterising neon sign in their heads that advertises: 'Vacancy. Winter rates'.

When Alexis and Nerida visited him, Constantin was always sitting in the same cane chair in the conservatory. Like a schoolboy delivering homework to a master, he would hand Alexis a sheaf of papers covered in dense, horizontally inclined handwriting, which Alexis flicked through, while nodding approvingly. Then with a courtly Middle-European bow, Constantin would leave the conservatory without attempting any conversation. Responding to Nerida's enquiries, Alexis said the work was good. Strange and lateral but lucid. He said he would file it against Constantin's return.

The abdominal pains were the fault of the carbamazepine. Alexis reeled out of the bathroom and regarded Nerida tenderly, curled up like a question mark in their bed. He did not care to be sick. Illness irritated him, profoundly. At four-fifty in the morning, the house was as unperturbed as a reservoir whose millions of litres leaked out a little at a time, without disturbing the surface. Unable to face his desk, he carried the file into the sitting room and placed it on the coffee table. He knocked back a shot of vodka. Feeling preternaturally calm to the extent of being detached from himself, Alexis opened the file, Constantin's file, and began to copy the salient points, because after all, the lectures were required, and like Drusilla, he hated waste and it was an act of friendship. Having crossed a boundary, Alexis looked back to see where he had come from but it was night-time and his vision wasn't good. He peered into the darkness. Hadn't Constantin given him this work unconditionally like an oblation or an exchange on a moonlit prairie where one brave, driven by the ties of kinship, gave up his soul to save the other?

As if he divined this, Constantin rose up to meet them for the last time in the conservatory, empty-handed. He had not spoken for three months, but now he giggled and declared that he had used up all his ideas. He kissed Alexis on the mouth and hugged Nerida so forcefully that she lost her balance. Restoring her to her feet, Constantin pointed at his temples with both index fingers and grinning widely, said, 'It's all gone. *Voilà*, I am happy. Do not come again. Me? I am refusnik!'

'What about Drusilla, Constantin? What about Linda?' Nerida protested. 'They love you.'

'Oh?' He made a great display of looking around gaudily like an actor in a pantomime. 'Where are they? On a high part of town, I think. Don't want to descend into the valley where this fog is thick and maybe criminals are hiding out. Not safe for pretty girls to go abroad at night.' Placing a finger in the centre of Nerida's forehead, he murmured, 'You women. So soft, but underneath . . . jackboot. You think you know what everyone is feeling. You think you are the commandant of the emotional concentration camp.'

'Go on, Constantin,' Nerida urged.

But his gaze wavered towards the ceiling, where trained jasmine clung to wires, and he shut his mouth, finally.

Constantin resisted contact and he resisted therapy. He resisted everything. He gave up and capitulated to his incubus, and said, what is the point of the so-called cerebral radiance? What happens if you refuse the gift? This is what happens when the gift overwhelms. I never asked for this. I will stay here for ever. Here is my cave, my exhausted mine.

Dearest Alexis

My coffee is growing cold. I am sitting in a restaurant with your letter in my hand and I am replying pronto, without any hello, how are you? or background detail about the weather and vibrant activities of San Cristóbal, because I have a bad, bad feeling. It's knotted up in your report about Constantin. I knew that would happen. I knew he would be lost. I have many private thoughts about Constantin which I can't talk about. What concerns me is this deceptively serene sentence here on the third page of your letter, where you say you are busy writing about An Ecological Approach to a Linguistic Problem and that your work is going well.

138

I don't believe you. Last night I woke from a dream in which you were performing an autopsy on Constantin. You removed the hippocampus.

Alexis, I know this is not your work. It's Constantin's. He and I, we talked about it in Paris in a haggard way. He was heading into the Gaia zone, linguistics as a science of myth. Please. Stop immediately or you will dilapidate yourself professionally. You won't be able to fake it. The source will be tracked down. Linda will find out, or one of Constantin's drinking companions of whom a number, being former fellow-travellers in the land of intellectual potential, would love to bring down one of their own, in order to soothe their ravaged egos. You are making a grave error of judgement which can only mean, despite all the jokes contained in your letter, that you are in some way desperate. Alexis! That is not you.

When I was in London, I saw the carbamazepine in your bathroom cabinet. I didn't speak to you about it because you did not initiate the subject of your epilepsy. But I'm saying to you now, give up that prescription. Your condition is not necessarily degenerative. You must know that a fear of seizures actually induces them. And stress exacerbates them. But in themselves, trance states – and I witnessed the genesis of yours – can be regarded as a privilege: the domain of artists and visionaries; the dynamo that sparks electricity. I believe it's your destiny to be entranced because that is how you have always asserted your genius. Shamans exist. Seers and psychics. It's just that in the overly rational Western world, those born with this gift tend to be slain by science, which becomes anxious and aggressive when faced by reverie. Trust me when I say this. I am a doctor! I've looked at both sides and I don't dismiss the out-of-the-blue.

It seems to me that you are thrashing around in a

limbo or trembling on a brink. Why don't you give up the medication and come to Mexico? I have been spending some time with Eugene, who always sends you his enthusiastic regards. His project here could use your collaboration and I know he has several times extended an invitation to you to work at the Ethnographic Centre. Why don't you do this? At the very least, for a change of scenery. At the very best, you will write your book. Toos de Bruin – a Dutch art dealer, who has lived in Chiapas for years – recalls meeting you in Los Angeles. You, and Nerida of course, could stay in her house.

Finally, I have to speak selfishly. I urge you to come here because it is ten years since we spent any length of time with one another, and I miss you. You are my brother. My blood. Haven't I always looked out for you? We are connected and interwoven, like warp and weft.

All my love, Dru.

Drusilla's words worked on Alexis like a slow-release tablet, invisibly reducing the fever of discontent and dispersing foul humours. He felt a sudden desire to play music at a volume that would disturb the neighbours. His appetite returned triumphantly. He considered running a marathon. Had a household altar been integrated into the Italian furnishings of the living room, he would have gratefully sacrificed a chicken, or more appropriately, have set a silk suit on fire, to honour Clotho, the Spinner, the eldest of the Moirae who determine the course of human life. Drusilla, extending a soft, sisterly hand – so longed for; so hard to achieve – had supplied him with direction. THIS WAY TO HEAVENLY DESTINATION.

Leaving the house, with his coat billowing heroically, Alexis sauntered out of Dover Square. Extravagant drifts of fallen leaves dragged at his ankles but he kicked them away. The leaves were so light and brittle, they were no obstacle at all, unlike impacted snow, which impeded progress and chilled the bones. Smiling at the prospect of a snowless winter, he began to walk more quickly, deftly cutting through the sluggish traffic in order to rendezvous with Nerida at The Oyster Bar, already anticipating the ejaculation of champagne into his glass. In his study, the carbamazepine lay at the bottom of the wastepaper basket where he had thrown it several days before, on receipt of Drusilla's letter, along with half a ream of misguided prose.

Two dozen oysters glistened on a crystalline bed of ice. Nerida squeezed lemon juice over them, which increased the oysters' liquid glare. Her eyes were tired after a week spent at the film co-operative running tests on stock, Agfa-Gevaert, Eastman Kodak and Du Pont. She had pushed stops and experimented with shifting colour values, looking for extreme effects, as, she was smart enough to realise, the novice does, hoping that wild saturation or high contrast or marks of static electricity on the film would substitute for thought. But she was happy. She was astonished at the difference between using a still camera and a movie camera. When she applied her Nikon, the world became frozen and enclosed and discrete. But the Bolex was unruly. She was compelled to link one image with the next, while contemplating the process. The difference between a snowstorm in a paperweight and the view from the Trans-Siberian express, which was very big with a teleological thrust.

Alexis was approaching. Threading his way through the candlelit restaurant, towards her. A tall slim man with a vivid face. He kissed her fingers and sat down and beamed approvingly at the champagne, the oysters, the thin slices of brown bread. The metres of his navy coat spilled on to the floor. Nerida brushed at his lapel.

'This is new.'

'I know. It's very *bonsoir*, Lord Byron. But I felt hyperbolical. You look beautiful. What happened in the darkroom?'

Nerida related her encounters with daylight and tungsten speeds, to which Alexis responded with exuberance. He touched her hand, her arm, her face. He was imperishable. She began to laugh for no reason at all and said, 'What? What is it? Something celestial?'

Alexis topped up her glass, controlling the champagne so that it did not surge over the rim. He said, 'Would you like to go to Mexico?'

'Mexico? For a holiday?'

'For the winter. For a break. We'd have somewhere interesting to stay and I would work. I am planning something.'

A microbe of disappointment swam into Nerida's mind – she had just connected with the film co-operative; she was intending to make a statement even though it was as yet unarticulated – but then it was eaten up by a huge emotion. Alexis. So I disappear in him and I would like to. He is like a maze, complicated and disciplined, designed for losing yourself in. When you can't find your way out, you take a novel from your bag and read until you are rescued. The birds continue to sing. The sun still shines.

Alexis removed a postcard from his pocket, and without showing it to her, said, 'I mentioned your talents to Eugene.' He read from the postcard: 'Delighted to hear that Nerida has a camera. This could be useful. Thinking of documenting some of my work on film. *Hasta luego.*'

'So we will go to Chiapas.'

'If you agree.' He paused and tore at the bread just as Drusilla had done in their kitchen. 'I have stopped taking the drugs. I want to recuperate.'

'I can't argue with that. What will you work on?'

'In the short term, Tzotzil grammar: alternative solutions versus weaknesses. And then, Zeugen.'

It pleased Nerida to see him so determined. Delicately, she clinked her glass against his. 'We'll go.'

Alexis raised himself from his chair, and leaning across the table, kissed her mouth, which, by focusing on a sensuous detail, diverted attention from the whole story. They were both slaves to sensation.

17

Alexis sat at a window table in the best café on the plaza in Oaxaca, reading about the Earth Lord, an overweight slug of a deity who made the people of Zinacantan toe the line. It was a fine, ordinary Sunday afternoon. An hysterical brass band played while dressed-up families promenaded in the November sunlight. Street-vendors sold corn, toffee apples, pastries, tamarind water, pralines, pecans, and hot tortillas wrapped around cooked meat. Everybody was eating, cramming dripping tacos into their mouths, gnawing on ears of blackened corn. Alexis stroked the calloused joint on the middle finger of his right hand. The deformity was caused by the continual pressure of a writing implement. His throat was protected by a silk scarf. He was saving his voice. Nerida and Drusilla drank pulpy margaritas out of shot glasses, while flicking through the magazines, *Vogues*, *National Geographics* and *Scientific Americans*, they had discovered in a second-hand bookshop.

Out of the corner of her eye, Nerida watched Alexis extract a notebook from his pocket. He uncapped his fountain pen. For some minutes his hand hovered over the page, the pen lolling between his fingers. Then he began to write. Nerida hummed along with the band and grinned at a shoeshine boy who wore a small green parrot on his shoulder.

'What's his name?' she called through the open window.

'Paco.'

She bought matches from a hunch-backed woman for the pleasure of speaking Spanish, although as Drusilla remarked, Spanish was probably not the match-seller's native tongue. Last night Alexis had slept peacefully, until just after dawn when the bells of the church, which was situated adjacent to their hotel, had begun to peal rapturously.

Their departure from Oaxaca was delayed by Drusilla's communion with local weavers. She had made an adventurous journey by bus from San Cristóbal to meet Nerida and Alexis, and also to repair an omission in her collection of Zapotec textiles. While Drusilla was absent, Alexis coolly bought, for cash, a red Dodge Pioneer because the car was ugly and unusual. Big fins, clunky round lights, showy dashboard. Weighed two and a half tons. The kind of car a man would drive. Parking it flamboyantly some distance from their hotel, Alexis had laughed at the folly of it. 'It's ridiculous,' he said, looping the rosary beads, which had come gratis with the vehicle, around the rear-view mirror. 'It's so dumb, it's perfect. What do you think?'

Nerida loved the car. 'It makes me feel impervious.'

'Steel chassis,' Alexis whispered. 'Like a halo. Oh, I feel good, Nerida.' He coughed. 'At least spiritually. What the hell is wrong with my throat?'

'You did talk about seven hours non-stop on the plane.'

'Uh-huh. I couldn't help it. Leaving London behind, it's like escaping a zero-gravity situation. I'd lost my grip on things. There was no grip. Now I'll drive. That's what I'd like to do.'

Their dusty Dodge roared along the precipitous, serpentine road leading to the market town of San Cristóbal de las Casas. Alexis was at the wheel. Despite the efforts of a ten-year-old gas station attendant and his all-purpose rag, the windscreen remained smeared with mashed yellow butterflies, a souvenir of Oaxaca. They were passing through highland Chiapas. A sacred volcano named Bankilal Muk'ta Viz, which contained the mythic secrets of the Zinacanteco world, rose from the difficult limestone terrain. But Nerida was looking at the photocopied notes in her hand. Eugene Rinehart's Tzotzil primer, a work in long, long, progress. Turning to Drusilla, she started to laugh.

'"His balls were wrecked by a bullet." And the next sentence is, "How do you feel now you are crazy?"'

'I think Eugene might be writing something witty in spite of himself.'

Nerida cranked the window open and let her yellow hair fly in the winter air. In the distance four Indian women filed along the edge of the road, their backs bent double under enormous baskets of maize.

'Look, Drusilla!' Drusilla was, in the name of a vacation, not attending births. The search for Mayan weaving and embroidery was ostensibly her reason for lingering in this region of Mexico. Satin. Fishbone. Stem. Running. Chain. Blanket. Feather. Cross. Long-armed cross. Herringbone. Plain couching. In Chiapas dogwood leaves, under the influence of alum or chrome, make yellow. Elaborate methods of styling hair exist. These rely on thick woollen cords or woven ribbons. The women usually go barefoot. This was the poetry of Drusilla.

The baskets were attached to tumplines which pulled taut and biting across the women's foreheads. Drusilla, nestled in the back seat of the Dodge among magazines, boxes of books and a tape recorder, craned her head but Alexis was already swinging around a curve in the road. The Indians were gone.

'It's bloody cold,' Alexis said.

Nerida stroked her fingers on the roof of the car, then wound up the window. She wanted to use her camera but it

146

was locked in the boot. Why had she put it there out of reach? Rinehart's Tzotzil primer slid from her lap. On one side of the road pine forest, interspersed with oaks, grew on the steep hills. On the other, the earth fell away for a thousand metres. They were now so high above sea-level that all the obvious images of Mexico had been left behind. All that hey, *chiquitita*, you wanna *mariachi* with me, all that sombrero kind of thing. Beyond Alexis's fixed profile, Nerida could see nothing but sky full of fluffy pastel clouds. If only she had remembered to carry the camera with her she would have something to do. And if she read more she might achieve an idea. Alexis and Drusilla were riddled with them.

Alexis was slowing down to negotiate a hairpin bend ahead. Clouds of dust obscured his vision. Watch out or you'll drive right off the edge. He had felt cold before with the window open but now his shirt was sticking to his back. His tongue was sandpaper. Felt like he was stranded in a hot, hot desert.

Nerida said, 'If a Zinacanteco has offended, the gods use a bolt of lightning to knock out the bad part of his soul.'

What was Nerida talking about? She doesn't know anything. This road like a fucking sandstorm. The Sudan, Ethiopia, Egypt. Driving through a sandstorm, under the influence of homicidal impulses, trying to find the Zar cult so he could be cured. Mmn, says the high priest or witch-doctor or Zar-father or whatever the hell he is, you've got the Zar sickness. Boy, time to bow down to the genies of the earth. Zar sickness tosses you back and forth between petrification and euphoria. But you're proud of this illness. The Zaree's suffering makes him special, spiritual. Other people better respect Zar or they might become infected themselves. Watch out.

'Alexis? Are you all right?'

'Shit.'

147

Coming out on to the straight, they were hard up against an ancient truck. The dusty tailgate bore the handpainted legend, in English, 'Speed King'. Its tray was packed with upright labourers, some holding machetes. A few of them grinned and some, spotting blonde Nerida, pointed and waved. Others directed a hostile stare at the vehicle now trapped in their wake. For several minutes the big car vibrated along the rutted road in second gear. The truck belched black exhaust fumes which infiltrated the Dodge, even with its windows closed. Alexis shook his head impatiently, then pulled out to overtake the truck. But the road was narrow and treacherous. He retreated, continuing at a crawl while the sun slowly sank. The prospect of a Mexican night drive was unpleasant.

Then a thin arm extended from the cab, waving them forward. Alexis hesitated, in the face of the collective challenge radiating from the tray. Nerida was dismayed. Machismo. The disembodied arm was making exaggerated sweeping movements as if to usher forward a timid child. The Dodge accelerated jerkily to the left, but Alexis seemed unable to free himself from the labourers' intense gaze. He fell back, resuming his checked position behind the truck. He was hunched over the steering wheel. A drop of sweat oozed from his hairline, slid over his cheek.

'I want to stop for a few minutes.' Nerida touched his leg. 'I need some air.'

'Toos is expecting us.' He would not look at her.

Climbing a hill, they rounded another chicane in reluctant tandem. The labourers appeared to be joking among themselves. Then one by one they turned their backs on the Dodge, anticipating their arrival home. Nerida was about to speak when the sudden gunning of the engine threw her against the door. Alexis spun the wheel, snaking the Dodge out and parallel to the truck. Their wheels caught the build-up of gravel adjacent to the precipice. The car swayed, then hurtled past the truck. Nerida registered a look of surprise on the face of the driver's mate. Simultaneously she was aware that the Dodge was speeding towards a blind rise.

In front of the truck they came across an unexpected Volkswagen. It shrank to the right as Alexis furiously accelerated past, through a wisp of clammy cloud on the road that chilled the air. Nerida felt dizzy. It's the altitude, the altitude, she kept repeating to herself as they flew over the crest and thank God, there was no approaching vehicle.

She was exhaling a long breath when she was puzzled by a blur of dark-green pines, no, the sky soaring by, immense, blank. For one heart-stopping instant the Dodge seemed to leap at the horizon. The sound of her mother singing rushed at her: 'Land, land, where the ladies sit with their gold combs in their hair/Awaiting for their own dear lords for them they'll see no more.' Home rushed at her. When she was six she had stood on a point where two oceans collided. Now she was glad she did not have any family left to burden with grief.

The Dodge continued its languid, deadly revolution for several centuries. Then skidded to a halt and stalled. The road to San Cristóbal lay before them.

Alexis turned the key and drove for a couple of minutes, before pulling the car over at the first appearance of a verge. 'Jesus. Maniac at the wheel.'

Drusilla groaned, pulling her *rebozo* over her head. But Nerida began to giggle, throwing her arm around Alexis's shoulder.

'Oh baby.' He gasped and coughed, grimacing at the tearing in his throat. Then he smiled. The Dodge drifted downhill, with Nerida clinging to him.

The sun slipped away, leaving a brief monochromatic twilight, as the Dodge lurched up Toos de Bruin's rocky driveway. Toos acted as a broker for artists in the south, connecting them with clients in search of ceramics, textiles,

149

tinware and paintings. Sometimes she rented rooms in her house to those whose company she might find agreeable.

Killing the engine, Alexis stretched his sinewy arms over his head. Dense trees stirred on the hills surrounding the L-shaped two-storeyed house. Shaky electric light burned in the tall windows, guarded by wrought-iron grilles, on the ground floor and flickered from lamps hanging in the arched entranceway. Striding to the passenger side, Alexis handed Nerida from the car. The night was damp and cold. She kissed his ear-lobe, glad that Drusilla was asleep among the books and magazines. The front door of the house was opened, releasing a faint aroma of charcoalled meat and a fluvial silhouette whom Nerida took to be Toos de Bruin.

Toos, accompanied by a great deal of fabric, ran down the shallow steps and offered her cheek for Alexis to kiss. She seized his arms. 'Alexis, you look terrible!' And peering over his shoulder at Nerida, 'What has this man been doing to himself?'

'Toos,' Alexis croaked, 'this is Nerida. Nerida, Toos de Bruin.'

Toos, whom Nerida judged to be in her late fifties, shook hands and said heartily, '*¡Esta es su casa!*' Nerida acknowledged the greeting with a small bow. Toos was tall. She wore a voluminous smock over what appeared to be several skirts. Her still fair hair was plaited and pinned to simulate a crown.

'We have been longing to meet you,' she murmured.

Nerida felt herself become insubstantial as Toos wrapped her in an embrace.

'Where's Gene?' Alexis whispered. Eugene was a research fellow at the Centro de Investigaciones Etnográficas in San Cristóbal.

'He sends apologies, but he's out in the field.'

Nerida was disappointed. She could see that Alexis was too. His face was stiff and white.

'He's back tomorrow or the day after. Drusilla! Here you are with all your treasures.'

Nerida watched Drusilla step from the car, her *rebozo* trailing attractively. She exchanged dignified kisses with Toos. A gust of wind whipped through the trees. At night the sky became a jaguar, its blue-black pelt marked by stars.

'Come, come,' Toos cried. 'Inside, everyone. Alexis, you want a chilli soup pronto for that cold. A good sweat is what you need. Where's Raúl? Raúl!' A slender young man sprang from the house. As he passed by Nerida, straightening his fitted white jacket, she saw that he was in fact middle-aged. Deep furrows ran from his nose to the corners of his mouth. While the Serafins extracted their hand luggage from the car, Raúl opened the boot and began to unload their cargo.

Toos decreed that the Serafins were shadows of their former selves. Ordering all excursions and projects to be suspended until Alexis's laryngitis had run its course, she had a bed made up for him in the ground-floor room which usually functioned as her office. Watched over by an old portrait of a younger Toos wearing Zinacanteca dress, her bony feet levitating above a field of flowers, Alexis lay propped on snowy pillows. Ancient issues of *Mexican Folkways* were to hand on the carved pine desk. Drusilla brought him cups of calming *té de manzanilla*. The weather was cold enough to produce several black frosts, whose iciness penetrated the thick walls of the house and crept over the floorboards and infiltrated the blankets on the bed where Nerida slept alone.

Alexis woke each morning to the swishing sound of the patio being swept clean. Through the window he observed Raúl snipping dead foliage from the dormant bougainvillaea which clung to one of the powdery walls enclosing the courtyard. He watched Graciela, Toos's muscular housekeeper,

151

beating the rugs. He slept a great deal. His body was weak, dissipated. His throat was still swollen. He could not speak but his mind began to blaze. Later Nerida thought that if she had been sleeping with him she would have noticed the first flicker of flame, like a candle accidentally knocked in the night against curtains which submit to the fire and suddenly the whole room is involved in a howling conflagration . . . But as it was, the molten glow in Alexis's brain went unremarked because all the damage was interior. Did you mistake me for the interpreter? Actually, I am Samuel Zeugen. That voice you hear is my voice. It's a hot afternoon in the kitchen during the first week of March. The sun has created a large white oblong on the wooden table. Mama is singing along to the radio while I lick the icing off a slice of coffee cake she has given me. My fingertips are buzzing. I'm so happy, happy, happy, happy and so alarmed that this feeling will flee into the past, which it must not do. This moment of love I must capture. I jump on my painted pony. Riding on the warpath to stop time. Naked and deadly. Going to risk my future. Danger. The thought of it makes me hard. I let go my arrow and it flies through the air. Imbeds itself in the heart of the recording angel. Angel falls in the dust. I snatch up his memories, his archives, his evidence.

18

Hearing a soft, rhythmic slap, slap, slap, which made her think of flesh and wet kid gloves being beaten against a marble counter, Nerida was drawn towards the kitchen. She had not previously entered this pungent precinct because it was guarded closely by Graciela, who saw herself as the grand vizier of the household. She was not to be crossed. More than once, Graciela had looked at Nerida with an expression that said, dismissively, you girl. Drusilla, on the other hand, Nerida noted with bemusement, was regarded as a woman, a *Señora*.

Driven by curiosity, Nerida pushed open the kitchen door, and found Drusilla and Graciela patting out tortillas, although this was not strictly necessary since a girl brought fresh tortillas to the house every day.

'Nerida! What are you looking for?' Drusilla's enquiry was civil, forestalling Graciela's inclination to shoo Nerida away.

'I wondered what the strange sound was.'

'There's coffee on the stove.'

While Nerida sipped sweet, acrid coffee, Drusilla, under Graciela's beady supervision, warmed the tortillas over an open flame. Her expression was meditative. Her skin gleamed. Whenever Nerida returned to the kitchen, she often discovered Drusilla there grinding onion, garlic and chillis in a mortar, or dropping dusty nuggets of black chocolate in a bowl of simmering milk, before whipping the mixture to a froth with the aid of a difficult wooden utensil. Sometimes Drusilla would ordain Nerida with a latent smile, which feinted at friendship. 'I like to do these things,' Drusilla said once. 'They are simple. You understand? You're a simple person, aren't you?' But mostly she didn't encourage conversation.

There was something conventual about those early days at Casa de Bruin, which were composed of silences, ritualistic meals and a lack of boisterous activity, at least until Toos returned in the evenings like a rally car set loose in Sunday traffic. Nerida was disconcerted by the static atmosphere of the house, which feeling surprised her, because she had always presumed that she was suited to an enclosed life. She attributed her gloominess to the fact that Alexis, who was her sun, was obscured by clouds. Nerida rose late in the mornings, without admitting to herself that she was happy to avoid breakfast with Drusilla, and dressed in a leisurely way, making every small action last a long time, as if the attachment of earrings or the pulling of a zip were significant. Below the bedroom window a young woman, who was never otherwise to be seen, pushed a broom up and down the patio, absorbed, as much as Nerida was, in the mundane.

When Nerida was presentable, she descended the curving stone staircase into the vaulted *sala*, whose high ceiling was supported by dark wooden beams. A central arch divided sitting room from dining room and in each area a pair of tall glassed doors led to the patio. Given Toos's penchant for complicated personal adornment, the *sala's* decor was restrained. Plain candelabra stood everywhere and above the dining table was suspended a wrought-iron chandelier so immense that the first time she sat beneath it, Nerida could not help directing fearful glances upwards anticipating a fatal crash.

The hearth was huge. Its firehood, stretching almost the entire length of the wall, was carved with a serpent frieze. An identical frieze was repeated on the hearth riser. From this fireplace there crept a delicious, tranquillising heat. Raúl would feed the fire, always seeming to bring in the wood when Nerida was present. This he would slowly deposit with a display of tight-trousered posturing. She ignored him and his heavy-lidded smouldering gaze, which she imagined he practised regularly in front of a mirror.

One afternoon, when the day was darkening, Nerida was lying, reading, on the sofa in front of the fire while Raúl crouched before the flames. The words, 'Remote Z-Men', suddenly wrote themselves into her mind. She lowered her book, envisioning a very useful alliance with Eugene Rinehart. Filming his subjects. Except that she would burst the bounds of documentary. She was eager for his return. And then she jumped, as a hand grasped her shoulder.

'Nerida . . .'

'God, Drusilla. I didn't hear you come in.'

Drusilla laughed. She was dressed in black with her plait hanging down. 'Sorry, but I could tell from right across the room that you were bored. Let me show you how to prepare the *nixtamal*.'

'*Nixtamal*?'

'Come on.' Her grip strong, she drew Nerida up from the sofa. As they entered the kitchen, Drusilla said, 'You have to cook the corn in lime and water to make the next day's tortillas.'

'Uh – huh.'

'You should know this. It's the way of life here.'

Drusilla's instructive tone irked Nerida, but she was also absurdly pleased that Drusilla was taking an interest in her, as if she were being given a special dispensation by a headmistress. The dried corn was soaking in a large

155

earthenware pot. Drusilla carefully crushed a lump of lime, transferred it to a container and covered it with a cup of cold water. Immediately the lime began to sizzle.

'Feel.' Drusilla took Nerida's hand and held it above the solution. A faint heat rose from the lime.

'It's burning.'

'Good. That's exactly how it should feel.' Drusilla placed the pot full of corn on the stove and dribbled into it a quantity of the limewater. She handed Nerida a wooden spoon. 'Stir.' The kernels began to change colour, becoming bright yellow. 'Now taste.'

Nerida sipped a little of the liquid from the spoon.

'How is it?'

'It bites a little bit.'

'Perfect. Now we wait a while.'

The two women stared at different things for several minutes, while the corn simmered. Nerida thought that Drusilla was one of the most powerful women she had ever met. Without speaking, she forced communication, but entirely on her terms. She was adept at intrigue. You did not walk out of the room because you were eager, in spite of yourself, to know what would happen next.

'I wouldn't have the patience to do this every day,' Nerida remarked eventually. 'It takes so much time.'

Drusilla pounced. 'And what is it that you are doing that is so much more productive?'

'I'm not telling.'

'Really? You have an undeclared ambition?'

Nerida felt compelled to admire Drusilla's complexity. While her mouth was uttering a sentence that veered ambiguously from insult to genuine interest, her limpid face was saying, so, impress me. To thwart that challenge, Nerida answered, truthfully, 'I don't understand the way you talk to me. I don't know what you think, whether you like me or not. Probably not. I don't know what to say to you.'

'If you have nothing to say, then we won't go very far. You are too sensitive, Nerida. But I like you very much. You're charming. You and Alexis make a handsome couple.'

'Thank you.'

But Drusilla didn't seem to hear. She was raising her soot-coloured skirt. Flicking an invisible speck of dust from her polished thighs, she regarded her legs thoughtfully and then slowly let the heavy cotton fall, apparently returning treasure to its hiding place. She smoothed the fabric with the tenderness of a caress and looked satisfied. 'I think maybe the corn needs another five minutes. You have to be patient.'

Drusilla shook the pan, then stood with her back to Nerida gazing out of the window. Being a refugee herself from the mirrored halls of mannerism, Nerida hoped that she and Drusilla might share an understanding, but she knew that the obstacle was Alexis. A car horn hooted in the distance, and then a grumbling engine and the sound of gravel being tortured by speeding wheels proclaimed Toos's arrival. Returning to the stove, Drusilla examined the corn and hefted the pot on to the bench.

'All ready for tomorrow. I think we could have a drink now.'

Drusilla and Nerida sat at each end of the sofa in front of the fire and accepted glasses of wine from Toos. Eugene Rinehart had not yet materialised.

'I can tell you why exactly,' Toos cried. 'To live with the Zinacantecos, Gene must drink. Then his head is so bad he can't get home. He tries hard to be the wild one. Ha! If you ask me, you have to be born to it.'

Thrusting her feet to the cold extremities of the bed, Nerida groped for her watch and was stunned to find that it was

157

a few minutes after one o'clock in the afternoon. Escaping from the sheets, she drew the weighty curtains. Clarifying sunlight shot into the room. The sky was hard and blue. The earth was red. Light shivered from the pine needles of the trees. Washing herself from the pitcher of water on the dressing table, Nerida noticed that the bruise on her upper arm, where she had fallen against the door of the Dodge, was finally beginning to yellow, but her arm still felt tender. It had hardly hurt at all at the time.

She came downstairs to find Alexis sitting at the lunch table, along with Toos and Drusilla, devouring a meal. Dressed in his recently adopted sleepwear of white cotton shirt and wide drawstring trousers, he looked like a peon enjoying a remission from the fields. She lightly kissed him and stroked his face.

'You're cured!'

'About time. I feel very well.' He was happy to be on his feet again. A man looks bad propped up on pillows, he thought. After his remedial week, he was in an attacking mood. His work. A man should work. (Although once, a distant voice cried, you didn't use this strident tone.)

Toos flapped a napkin at Nerida. 'You sleep like a baby, Neridita. *Muy bien.* You get old like me and there you are tossing and turning half the damn night. Sit down and eat.'

Nerida dropped into a chair, smiling at Alexis.

'So now Alexis is restored,' said Toos, 'we'll have a very big dinner tonight and open the wine you brought. It's too late for the market now but I can get chickens from Maria-Luisa if she has made up her fight with Graciela.'

When Graciela came to clear the plates away, Toos harassed her into making a fresh pot of coffee, then made preparations for departure. On her way out she dumped several American newspapers on the table, for Alexis to read after lunch. Drusilla declined to accompany Toos on her errands. Instead

158

she settled on the sofa with Alexis and began recounting her kitchen experiences at Casa de Bruin, reminding him of culinary episodes, some supreme and others catastrophic, from their shared past, while Nerida photographed them for the record, happy to be on her feet. As a girl, she had been a terrific runner and there had been nothing to compare with the fleeting touch of bare feet on the grass of the primary-school field, her ponytail thumping between her shoulder-blades, herself a blur of concentration and effortless command of her body. She had been a sprinter, so no tactics were involved. Only speed. She would say to Eugene, although based on anthropological reality, it will be a fictitious film fizzing with the *joie de vivre* of imagination. Called to the open air, Nerida left through the french doors, waving a silent farewell to Alexis and Drusilla who were covertly weeping over deceased things, while pretending to laugh.

A large tree – Nerida didn't know its name – grew in the courtyard, throwing complex shadows over the turquoise-and-green tiles on the inoperative wall fountain opposite the *loggia*. Nerida strolled towards the fern-lined archway that would take her past the vegetable garden and the well, which also functioned as an al fresco laundry, and up the hill to a wilderness.

She stepped through the arch. Some fifteen metres distant, a sandy-haired man stood with his back to her. He was facing a grove of citrus trees, his hands on his hips in an attitude suggesting exasperation. Waiting furiously for reluctant fruit to fall. Eugene Rinehart. He called something, and called again. Nerida hesitated, feeling she had stumbled upon an intimacy. He bowed his head abjectly. Determined to manage their introduction with finesse, she decided to retreat to the house until he chose to make an official appearance. But immediately he swung round, and froze at the sight of her. Nerida waved. Casting a glance over his shoulder, he walked diffidently to meet her.

She stretched out her hand. 'Dr Rinehart?' She knew neither of them would mention the Lenox.

'Oh,' he gasped. 'Please. Eugene. You're – ah – Nerida.'

She nodded, smiling. He was short, a dumpling, and did not know what to do with his glasses, which he removed and replaced twice in the awkward minute they stood there by the vegetable garden. The most striking thing about him was the injury to his face. His right cheek was bruised. A long, thin cut ran across it.

'I've been looking forward to meeting you.'

'Really. Me too. I was out in the field.' He made a sudden flourish with his glasses, blinking in surprise when they flew from his grasp.

'That's OK. Toos explained. Actually Alexis has been in bed all week with laryngitis.' She noticed, as he picked up his glasses, how he smoothed the seat of his trousers in an automatic attempt to diminish his plump backside. This gesture drew her sympathy. Eugene might yet be a catalyst. It was not his fault that she placed such importance, as Alexis did too, on beauty and style.

'Toos is out!' Nerida cried. 'But Alexis and Drusilla are at home. They'll be delighted to see you.'

They began to walk back to the house. Eugene was wearing a pair of moccasins that reminded her of slippers, pipes, and dressing-gowns. Beauty and style. They converted circumstance into opportunity and avenues, tree-lined boulevards of escape. What messenger from the fates seeking to cultivate a face in the crowd would choose a plain person?

'I kind of had an incident.' Eugene touched his face.

'What happened?'

'Well.' He grew lively. 'I'm at a village, a hamlet really, with Lol Perez and – '

160

'Eugene!' Drusilla emerged from the french doors. 'Where have you been?'

'Don't worry. You'll hear. It's great to see you, Dru.' He kissed her cheek. 'Lexie!' Eugene clapped Alexis on the back and wrung his hand.

'Good. You've met Nerida. How are you, Eugene? What happened to your face?'

'Oh it's nothing,' Eugene said proudly.

They returned to the sitting room. 'What can we get you?' Drusilla asked. 'Are you hungry?'

Eugene struggled out of his jacket. His denim shirt was very stained. 'Nothing right now. I'd like to freshen up. And I need a nap. I can't tell you what a week I've had.' Backing away, Eugene raised his hand. 'Hey, it's terrific to see you, Lexie. We'll catch up at dinner, OK.'

'I'll look forward to it.'

As Eugene bounded up the stairs, Drusilla raised her eyebrows at Alexis, and directed at him a message which said, we can't help being superior. And Nerida thought: Drusilla could bring out the worst in Alexis, which hardly seems right, since she should be a reminder of love. But, in her presence, I can see it! He becomes weak and abject.

19

The plumbing had seized, but the Serafins didn't mind. These recalcitrant pipes confirmed the caprice of Mexico. Raúl began making repairs, leaving Graciela to stagger upstairs with buckets of hot water. She refused all offers of help, while rolling her eyes dramatically to communicate the agonising weight of her burden.

Even on a sunny day the upstairs bathroom was frigid. Ultramarine tiles covered every surface, with the exception of the ceiling. A naive mermaid was painted on the wall above the bathtub. Since Nerida felt the cold, Toos had ordered a kerosene heater to be lit, after castigating Raúl for not having done it earlier. Nerida stood at the washbasin, brushing her fine hair. Crackling with static, it flew everywhere at each stroke of the nylon hairbrush. Through the speckled mirror she watched Alexis enter, carrying properly effective American towels, which he threw on to a rusting chair.

'You're pleased to see Eugene?'

'Naturally.' He undressed. He mistook her silence. 'You weren't impressed.' He caught up one of the still steaming buckets and stepped into the mouldy, high-walled bath.

'I wasn't repelled by him. He does interesting work, doesn't he? He's got a mind.'

Loading the ocean sponge with water, Alexis began soaping his body in his usual systematic way. 'He's an innocent. Transparent.' Alexis drenched his hair, passing the sponge over his mouth, his nose, closing his eyes, narrow and dark like Drusilla's, sweeping back his hair. Nerida handed him the shampoo, which he dripped into the palm of his hand. He lathered his hair. 'You won't be bored here, will you? I shall be out and about with Eugene.'

'Of course I won't be. I've got things to do.'

'How are you getting on with Drusilla?' He was rinsing his hair.

'Like chalk and cheese. Like iron filings to a magnet. I don't know. I like her, Alexis, but – she's really hard to figure out. Anyway, I envy your connection with her, because I haven't got any family.'

Alexis was pouring the remaining water over his head. It sluiced down his chest.

'It's true, she's my only family. I need a towel.'

Nerida brought him a towel, and while he scrunched it over his head, she covered his nipple with her mouth and her tongue flickered.

'Yes,' he said. 'Do that.'

In the bedroom, Nerida peeled off her clothes as fast as she could. Her moving limbs threw elongated shadows on the walls. Alexis had not completely closed their door. She caught a glimpse of Drusilla entering the room opposite theirs, also leaving her door open. A cast-iron stove crouched by the door but it was not in working order. Shivering, Nerida wound her arms around Alexis. He lifted her up and they fell on the bed. Drusilla, Nerida thought with a guilty stab of satisfaction, would be sinking on to her bed with a copy of the essay Eugene had so thoughtfully urged upon her on the stairs. Alexis sucked Nerida's tongue into his mouth. He smoothed her body with his hands, pressing her into the soft bed. He bit her feet, the sensitive flesh of her instep. He gathered her up. I am not the kind of woman, Nerida thought with gratitude, who sits alone reading 'The Evolution

163

of the Tense-Aspect System of Tzotzil and Tzeltal Mayan'. With a footnote thanking Dr A. Serafin for his stimulating contributions.

Alexis sat up and looked at her. 'What are you thinking of?'

'Myself. Vain, vain thoughts.'

He fell back on his elbows, collapsed on to his back. She loved him naked, loved him essential. Loved his scalp and his shoulders. If only she were strong enough to pick him up and run away with him, because something black and crushing was rolling towards them. A stone turning into a boulder turning into a rocky enormity. Nerida crawled towards him and took him in her mouth. She was lying on his legs, one hand beneath her forehead resting on his stomach. His muscles contracted. She was constant but she wouldn't go fast because she didn't want this to end, not yet. Then he lifted up her head, aching for her, kissed her mouth, turned her over and thrust deep into her. Moved up and down very slowly, erasing that sick moment of apprehension.

Alexis took care. He submerged his face in her hair. After this, things will never be the same. He could not stop thinking. Was it too much to ask to drown in her? He wanted to, wanted that peace, but he kept rising to the surface. He paused and laid her on her back again.

'How long will this last?' He spoke tenderly because he didn't want to alarm her.

He rocked back and forth on her, for ever. She was supine on the veranda while the sun passed overhead from east to west, gradually creeping beneath the overhang. Hot light fell on to her feet and by degrees inched up her legs, exposing her to an increase of heat. It stole over her body until it reached her face. She shut her eyes against the brightness. Tears started in them. Sighs flew out of her mouth. Thoughts hurled themselves through Nerida's brain in a fleeting subdivision of time: winged thing. Axiom. Synthesis. Ecstatic generalisation. This must mean something – this sensational accuracy; this erasure; this love, love, love, love.

And Alexis thought: It's an orgasm. It's a physiological function. And I have flaws, personal flaws, to overcome. This cannot be the centre, this love, love, love, love: it drives me crazy.

Pulling the heavy blankets over themselves, they lay close for a long time. Then Alexis slid his fingers inside her again because he could not leave her alone, and he kept his fingers there. 'Sweet thing.' He closed his eyes. He murmured, 'Nerida is alive. I love you.'

While Toos and her guests ate chicken with herbs and beans, Alexis described hilariously their travels south. Nerida and Drusilla laughed as hard as the others, although Drusilla did once shoot an ironic glance at Nerida, relieved that the sometimes tense journey had been translated into an amusing experience. In deference to Toos's prior sartorial claim on indigenous Mexico, Drusilla had put aside her tribal items for vaguer garments. This evening she wore a severe, dark-red velvet dress. From time to time she plucked at the sleeves and rearranged the folds of the skirt as if she were dissatisfied. Alexis's reportage was so torrential, it was not until they had finished the main course that Eugene, who had already made two or three failed attempts to divert attention to himself, was able to tell why or how he had been wounded.

'So I was returning to the hamlet with Lol Perez and night was coming on. He was telling me this story about a man on his way back from the lowlands. When it got dark this guy tied up his mules and settled down to sleep. Seems he had a bad feeling though, so he slept with his gun at his side. Then just before dawn he woke up and saw a ghost mooching round.'

'What did the ghost look like?' asked Nerida.

'I guess like a man. Like anything you want. So this man blasts the ghost with his gun, but even though he's pumping these bullets right into the thing's chest, he couldn't kill him. The ghost just says, "What did you do that for? I could give you a lot of money." "OK," says the guy, *muy bien.*" So the ghost hands over the money and then the guy fires one more bullet at the ghost and this time, the ghost dies.

'Now the man notices that the ghost has wings on his ankles, so he breaks them off and sticks them on his own feet. He rises up in the air and goes swooping around the mountains and eventually flies home and this guy, he's a real hero. Everybody still talks about him. If you can stand up to a ghost and shoot him down then you get rich and you've got the power to fly. Lol says that's the way the story was left. Everybody still talks about it. I'm collecting a lot of these stories. It takes some drinking to do it, but hell, you do what you have to do.'

'How did the cut happen on your face? It wasn't a ghost.'

'Lol had just finished this ghost story when suddenly this hail of stones is launched at us. Lol threw himself on the ground like he was expecting it but me, I was like, what? huh? and this big stone hits me on the cheek. Lol's lying on the ground kind of angry but also laughing up a storm. It seems that the ambush is because of a feud between himself and his brother-in-law.'

'How serious a feud?' asked Drusilla. 'Did they mean to kill him, or just create some superficial damage?'

'Probably kill him,' said Toos. 'These aren't half-hearted people.'

'Yes, they would kill him and then there'd be something to talk about. Something big.' Alexis was pouring more wine.

'According to Lol, if I hadn't been there, the machetes would have come out. So we have a drink and set off again. I tell you, it's really black out there on those tracks at night. Then Lol says he guesses the machetes would come out anyway before we reached home. It seemed like a very long walk.'

'So now you're one of the protagonists in a local anecdote,' said Alexis.

'I've been around so long, I guess they've been gossiping about me all this time. I hope so.'

'Mmn. It would be depressing to be unworthy of gossip.' Drusilla's tone was just dry enough to extinguish Eugene's smile.

'What are you looking for, Eugene?'

'Well, Nerida, maybe gossip is a misleading word. It's not just yak-yak-yak. It's my access to, to – it illuminates the whole structure of the Zinacanteco world. It's a, it's like a moral universe. I don't know what I'm going to do when I finish my book. A regular teaching job, I guess. Grading assignments. Sitting on your ass all day with a pen in your hand.' Eugene whipped off his glasses. 'That's no work for a man.'

'Writing is not inherently dangerous,' said Alexis. 'Unless one chooses to make it so.' He wanted to leap from a building and defy death and live to write something bloody and blasting about it. He hated this storm, this cancelling sandstorm that was sweeping through him, because, unlike his days of trances, he did not know when it would blow itself out. And it came out of nowhere. During hors-d'oeuvres he had been serene. Suddenly he was not. Most depressing of all, Nerida became not enough. Even though he could lie full-length in the dirt and kiss the footprints she had made . . . How could you love a woman utterly and still, it wasn't enough? Alexis poured himself a finger of mescal. It tasted like liquid ashes. It hit him in the back of the head. Good. He needed Eugene.

Toos yelled, 'Graciela!' Then she swept Eugene's topic away. 'Writing. Poof! Travel is the good thing. You should move around while you're young. Something will happen. When I was a girl I never went out of my town. But when I married Joop, they sent us everywhere. He was a surveyor, you see. First we were in Indonesia and after that Guyana. Finally we came to Chiapas. I loved this place the moment I laid eyes on it and I knew I was home.' She nodded approval as Graciela delivered wobbly custard flans to the table.

Alexis said, 'You're trying to blend in, Gene. That's not possible. Why not take a more radical position? Intervene. Don't you think that to know a reality you must transform it?'

Nerida was listening. Something hazardous was going on here.

'I'm hearing ego speaking, Lexie.' This from Eugene.

'Well, why not? We're all looking inside. We're all fucking interior. We all make ourselves sick of our selves. Why don't you set people up against their expectations? Make them play a familiar game but change the rules.'

'I don't think that applies to a cogent culture – '

'Forget fucking cogent cultures for a moment. Excuse my language, Toos.'

'Say what you like. Just eat the flans. Graciela made a big fuss about them.'

'Go to a restaurant and act like you've got a complaint to address to a bank manager. Orientate a group of med students into the fine arts faculty. Use your imagination.'

Eugene looked puzzled as if he'd locked his imagination away in a box and only took it out on Sundays and public holidays.

'It's what the Russian formalists called "making strange",

Gene. It's novelty or newness as a source of aesthetic value. When you make something ordinary strange, by placing it in a different context, you bring new life to the hierarchy.'

'But I don't have anything to do with the ordinary. I work with the exotic.'

'I know. Toos, bail me out here. Change the subject.'

Eugene said, '"Making strange". I'll make a note of that.'

'What can I tell you? When Joop retired, he wanted to go back to Holland. By this time I already had this beautiful house. So, I let him go. Go on, eat. There's fruit too. So he has a heart attack in a coffee house in Delft.' She sighed and ate a mouthful of flan.

Eugene was sitting opposite Nerida, facing the door to the kitchen. He was raising a spoonful of custard to his mouth when he saw something over Nerida's shoulder that made him stare. He lowered his spoon.

'What do you know?' Toos went on. 'Dead. If I'd gone back there what would they have thought of me in Delft?' She held up her strong tanned arms and jangled her bracelets. 'Ridiculous! Completely out of place!'

An Indian servant entered the room carrying a large plate of nuts and dried fruit. She was young, with chiselled features and a lugubrious expression. Pink satin ribbons were woven into her long thin plaits. She was distracted in her movements as if her mind were elsewhere.

Eugene said suddenly, 'Xunka!'

But the woman did not acknowledge him. Eyes lowered, she dumped the plate forcefully in front of Drusilla. Eugene uttered something, but the servant was already hurrying back to the kitchen. Eugene turned to Toos.

'When did she turn up?'

'Graciela tells me she just came into the patio so we gave

169

her some work. I don't know how long she is staying. You know what she is.'

'Who is she?' Nerida asked.

'Oh Eugene wanted to find her work. She had some family troubles.'

'And you were speaking to her in Tzotzil?'

Eugene nodded. He stared anxiously at the closed kitchen door.

'Nerida's a great fan of your work. Did you know?' Drusilla was silky. 'Your manuscript was hardly out of her hand all the way here.'

Eugene squared his shoulders, then said quickly, before he lost the floor, 'Great! I'm flattered. It's designed to be a popular work. I mean obviously Berlitz won't ever bring out an edition, but, you know . . .' He laughed apologetically.

'Tzotzil,' said Alexis, 'is not a language in which one asks for a room with a view. The thing that interests me – and Eugene – is its capacity for describing errors.'

'Its moral vigilance,' added Drusilla.

'Exactly. Particularly where indiscretion, or even plain stupidity, is concerned.'

Nerida glanced at Eugene. It's not fair, his fixed smile said. This is my patch. The Zinacantecos are mine. But Alexis was immediately aware of his appropriation. 'God knows why I'm going on about it. Eugene is far more knowledgeable than I about these lies and lapses.'

Conversationally, Eugene then became a waterfall. Unstoppable. Crashing on and on. It was nice to look at for ten minutes and take a photograph, but then you wanted to go somewhere urban for coffee.

'. . . and the aim is to record as many local stories as I can. To get an idea of their preoccupations and how their language is conditioned by social aspects. In the beginning it was tough getting anyone to talk to me. But I've learnt

Tzotzil and formed relationships. The biggest problem was that when the men did come to the Centre it wasn't a situation, you know, sitting around drinking, shooting the breeeze, where they felt like they wanted to talk. So what I do is I write down on index cards the names of various well-known men from around the hamlets. The men in the session select a name and try to write down all the anecdotes, or tell them to me, they can recall featuring that particular person. Once they get started the stories come pouring out and I get them on tape. Lexie has volunteered to help.'

'Simply as an interested observer,' Alexis added. 'I make a few notes, but it's all Gene's parade.'

Toos and Drusilla sat close together examining an old picture book of local costumes, many of which, it seemed from Drusilla's soft cries of distress, were now extinct. A jaunty *mariachi* record played in the background. Nerida's eyelids were heavy, but she was struck sufficiently by the warm halo surrounding Toos to ask, suddenly, 'Toos? You never had children?'

'Oh, you know – ' Toos twisted her rings. 'One stillborn. One taken by malaria. After that I didn't have the heart to try again.'

Nerida reached across and squeezed Toos's shoulder. 'I'm very sorry.'

'Me too. It was my fault. Usually the wives would go back home to have their babies. But I thought: What's good enough for the local girls is good enough for Toos. And it was. Alexis! It's bedtime for this girl.'

Alexis was fondling her cheek. Nerida sat up straight. Smoke plumed from the candles extinguished by Toos and Drusilla. The room was dim.

'We'll make an early start, Lexie.' Eugene yawned.

171

'Where are you going?' Nerida asked as Alexis helped her up.

'To the Centre. We're taking in the tape recorder.'

A commotion of jewellery occurred as Toos waved an extravagant good-night to the company. '*Buenas noches*, my friends.'

They bade her good-night and straggled to the staircase. Nerida lagged behind, letting Drusilla and Alexis go up first. Eugene, abruptly remembering his manners, leapt back so that Nerida might precede him. He trod heavily on her foot.

'Pardon me!'

'Don't worry. I'm fine.' But he looked so stricken that she sought to alleviate his discomfort by placing herself in his power. 'Actually, Eugene, I haven't had a chance to ask you – '

Eugene blinked rapidly and folded his arms. A man prepared for an onslaught. His eyes flicked to the top of the stairs. He was making her feel she was in his way.

'You know I have a camera. A movie camera.' Eugene nodded, staring at the fascinating floor. 'I think you mentioned to Alexis that you were interested in filming some of your people or – well, I'm not sure what exactly. Perhaps you were after some sort of record.' Nerida smiled her best smile.

'Ah yes. I did have a thought in that direction. Ha ha.'

'We could talk about it tomorrow if you like. Arrange something. I'd be happy to shoot some material for you. I could have the footage developed and edited in Mexico City.'

Eugene removed his glasses and squinted at the ceiling. After a moment he asked, 'What kind of camera?'

'A Bolex. Sixteen millimetre.'

'Uh-huh.' His glasses were back in place. 'Works off of batteries?'

'No, it's hand-wound. It's pretty old, but it's reliable. It's a beautiful camera; a classic. And for shooting here, I mean in uncertain conditions, it's an advantage not to have to lug batteries around or worry about temperature changes.'

'So you only get – what? A twenty-, thirty-second shot?'

'That's right. Twenty-eight seconds in fact. So you make allowances.'

'Uh-huh. Correct me if I'm wrong, but we're talking about a system that doesn't shoot sound?'

'That's right.' Nerida suddenly felt herself to be compromised by an enormous oversight.

'So you see the problem. I'm dealing with language.'

She was astonished that she had not taken this fact into account during her fantastic projection of a collaboration with Eugene. Swiftly she sought to convince him. 'But it will accept a motor. I could find one. I could get one with a sync-pulse and hook it up to a Nagra and shoot with sound.'

Eugene shook his head slightly. 'Oh there's no need to go to that trouble. You're here on holiday. Don't worry about it.'

'What about village life? A visual record?'

Eugene stepped aside, encouraging Nerida to take the stairs. 'That's a very complex proposition. You have to spend a long time in the field before shooting even one frame of film. You don't know these people. You can't just turn up, violating their community with your camera.' His tone indicated that any further discussion was purely academic. 'Well!' He clapped his hands together. 'Better hit the sack.'

'Of course. Good-night.' Remote Z-Men overheated and melted into inflammatory nothingness, as if she'd made the mistake of shooting on dangerous, fugitive nitrate stock, which no one in her right mind used any more. Nerida quickly climbed the stairs towards Alexis and their bed, where talk was not a prerogative.

20

Having kissed both Nerida and Drusilla, Alexis emerged from Toos's house into the invigorating open air. Eugene, hunched at the wheel of the rumbling Volkswagen, was impatient to leave for the Centre. Alexis paused and raised his hand to his throat. He had forgotten his scarf. Irritated, he shook his head. A scarf, for God's sake. Makes a man look like an invalid or a theatre director. He didn't need it. He was cured. His voice sounded normal once more. But suddenly Raúl was hovering at Alexis's shoulder, holding in his hands a neatly folded square of silk. To any observer, including himself, Alexis appeared to be a glossy example of a man in his prime who, although having recently taken a step backwards because of a minor illness which could happen to anyone, was now about to make up for lost ground. He had shaved closely. His clothes were calm and pressed. He was on his way to work. But these superficial repairs were hopelessly inadequate. Alexis could not see how deeply his personality had been corrupted by his long-suppressed desire for grandeur; that years ago the mechanism of his brain had slipped a cog, causing damage that had never been properly mended. The unruly contents of his cortex began to spin out of control, shredding in the teeth of its machinery the last remnants of rational thought. Now nothing strange seemed strange.

Raúl was staring into Alexis's eyes, while offering the scarf.

This exchange took only a few seconds, but it seemed to Alexis that Raúl was saying, ventriloquially: Boy, you're in a bad way. Could I interest you in a few local remarks on subjects close to you?

I'm close to Nerida. I'd like to live in a far-flung place with her and achieve something monumental.

So here you are. Between petrification and euphoria. You've come down with the Zar-sickness, no?

No! I'm extremely healthy and happy.

I don't think so, *profesor*. I see that sickness hanging like a bat. It likes the dark.

What remedies do you suggest?

When winding the string around your head, tie reef-knots at close intervals to make sure your thoughts are firmly under control:

Do not sit in the *zócalo* waiting for Z to approach or you will find yourself sitting there a long time, alone.

Regarding the girl, be most vigilant not to unplait her hair.

Regarding love, drive carefully here. If you fail to love adequately you will be hunted down and killed so skilfully you may not realise you're dead. OK, Señor?

Next thing: self. Love of ornamentation leads many people to further embellish selves already replete with woven or embroidered motifs. Please take this point, *gracias*.

On the subject of pools, it is all right to lean over the edge only. A sister cannot be relied on to rescue more than one child.

Those tormented by paper may find the following effective: fold the paper when damp and leave under a heavy weight for several days. When time has passed the paper may be worn as a skirt that lies flat at the front but is thickly pleated behind. This skirt is not easily lifted.

Eugene, who was eager to ride the range, even though his saddle-bags were stuffed with unmasculine magnetic tape and professorial pencils, tooted the horn. 'Lexie! Let's move!'

'Thank you, Raúl.' Taking the scarf, which wilted in his hands in the manner of silk, Alexis entered the car and gratefully settled himself next to Eugene, who was not given to extra-sensory exhortations. The VW bumped down the driveway, weaving elaborately between the potholes to protect the typewriter on the back seat from derangement.

Nerida stood on the grassy rise above the citrus grove, fixing her camera to its tripod. Already busy hands had been at work scrubbing laundry, judging from the evidence around the well. Two buckets and a scrubbing board and brush were lying by a zinc basin that stood on a drenched stone slab. Recently spilt water had coloured the earth black. From this spot she had a view of the patio. She saw that the kitchen door was open.

A caterwauling sounded from the house. Two figures appeared in the doorway, Graciela shoving Xunka into the courtyard. Graciela disappeared momentarily and then articles of sodden laundry hurtled from the door, landing around the feet of the girl. Graciela was yelling invective.

Xunka stood dumbly for a moment then dashed from the patio, through the arch and tore up the slope, clutching her long indigo skirt around her knees. At the sight of Nerida she hesitated, panting, and then struck out immediately for the ridge. Nerida took a picture of the girl just before she hurtled over the horizon. She felt a swirl of satisfaction at the simplicity of it. No assistants, no set-up, no cajoling of circumstances. Instead, a pentecostal call-and-response between hand and eye.

Nerida found San Cristóbal to be humane and picturesque, bathed in mountain air, embraced by hills. The town had the

177

exceptional atmosphere of altitudinous settlements, stranded and self-absorbed. The streets were filled with slow-gaited but purposeful people, Indians from the rural hinterland, mestizos and the occasional alien. Everywhere there were intensely curious children. An English-language school had recently opened, along with an annexe where weaving and claywork were to be taught in the summer months and an arts centre was in development.

Toos cited these examples of creeping civilization with some regret as they strolled from the bank, where Nerida had finally succeeded in changing money. Delighted to be out of the house, she resolved to put the blighted conversation with Eugene to one side. Careless to daydream; useless to brood. Toos's eccentric appearance provoked smirks from a group of young American tourists who did not see that she brought money to town; that she belonged to Chiapas; that she was the mother of dead children.

While Drusilla walked, she read a pamphlet about weaving given her by Toos. Miraculously she avoided all obstacles in her path. Without looking up from the page, Drusilla halted, like a bat conforming to its sonic radar, next to Toos's station wagon and wordlessly allowed Nerida to open the front passenger door for her. Toos gave the engine plenty of gas. The car strained at the kerbside for a moment, roaring painfully, then shot into Avenue General Utrillo. Toos, who encompassed the baroque, rococo and neo-expressionist schools of driving, expertly dodged unpredictable pedestrians and wandering mules, her touch light on the wheel. She wore at least half a dozen onyx rings. Glancing in the rear-view mirror, Toos's eyes intersected with Nerida's.

'You are too pale, Neridita. You must ask Graciela to make you *pozole*. It's a broth, very comforting, with pork and vegetables.'

178

'I'm terrified of Graciela. This morning I heard her having a screeching altercation with that girl Xunka about the laundry.'

'Washing clothes is important. Xunka knows that. You can be punished for going about in dirty clothes.'

'By whom?'

Toos threw up one hand. 'A Zinacanteca is responsible for clean clothes. Not in my house, necessarily, but as a rule. Xunka, she was in trouble at home. She's from Xul Vo. Eugene doing good works is how she came to us. It was all arranged through the *cabildo*, the town hall in Zinacantan. I don't know, she's just a bad one, always in trouble. Maybe they should send her to the curer. To the shaman.'

'What kind of trouble?'

'You must ask Eugene. He knows all the gossip.' Then Toos halted the car in the vicinity of the market. Nerida and Drusilla alighted and watched Toos accelerate away. They found themselves standing next to an Indian weaver, whose backstrap loom was tied to the radiator grill of a truck. The tiny woman, bowing over the loom, was absorbed in her work. A shawl, tied around her body, bulged at her back where a baby slept. She bent forward to pass the shuttle through the threads then leaned back firmly until the loom was tense. She slammed down the batten – *chock!* – then forward again to feed the loom. Drusilla stood very still, watching. Smoothly the weaver rocked back and forth from her hips, the movement punctuated by the heartbeat of the batten, the cloth imperceptibly growing like a living thing.

'They call the cloth a child of the moon,' Drusilla remarked in her typically lacquered way.

Nerida and Drusilla occupied a table in the market and ordered bright-orange carbonated drinks. Everywhere there were tousle-headed babies slung on their mothers' backs. Mournful ballads echoed from loudspeakers fastened to the

179

corrugated-iron awnings. Women draped in blue shawls sat behind small, neatly arranged pile of fruit and vegetables, white onions, chillies, cabbages, potatoes. Much of the produce was pathetically withered, but the vendors continuously sprinkled water over their harvests to make them look as inviting as possible. Two Chamula men stopped near Nerida's table and began haggling over the price of a chicken, its wings dripping blood.

'What do you intend to do with yourself?' Drusilla asked.

'You mean right now?'

'I mean with your life.'

'I don't have an intention. You're always asking me that.'

'Because I'm terribly interested in you.'

As usual Nerida could not decide whether this remark was sincere or sardonic, and as usual, she took a perverse pleasure in Drusilla's ambiguity because it acted as a little torment which Nerida felt she deserved. Watching the sinuous movements of Drusilla's fingers as she re-hooked an earring in her lobe, Nerida tried to imagine those hands slippery with blood and mucus, performing medical miracles and intimacies; but this aspect of Drusilla, like so many others, remained under wraps. She never volunteered anecdotes about her occupation; never made an observation that sprang from her clinical or cultural experience of childbirth on packed-earth floors or consultations undertaken in shaky territories plagued by civil wars.

'I never think of you as a doctor,' said Nerida. 'You don't ever talk about it.'

'What would you like to know?'

'Why did you choose medicine?'

'Because I was capable of it. Because it was the last thing my family expected of me.'

'What did they expect?'

'Nothing. Replication.'

'Did your parents –?' But before Nerida could embark on the interrogation that was close to her heart – the childhood of the Serafins, or more particularly Alexis – Drusilla expertly advanced the secondary subject.

'And then you are going to ask me, why bush medicine? The honest answer is ego. I liked the idea of being the last resort. I liked the idea of being everything – the consultant, the emergency ward, the generic woman attendant. That's all there is to say about it.'

'But that's heroic.'

'No it isn't. I don't even need the money, meagre though it is. I may not go back to it. I like it here. It's a long time since Alexis and I have been together.'

'Do you resent my presence?'

Drusilla laughed. 'Now why would I resent you, Nerida?'

'Because I'm with Alexis.'

'Does that mean he's cut off from all other communciation?'

'No!' Nerida felt tawdry. 'I'm just trying to understand you.'

'There's no need to burst a blood vessel over it. We don't have to exchange confidences. I'm on vacation.' Drusilla's gaze fastened on a couple trailing by, he carrying a piglet, she supporting a covered load on her back and a baby on her hip. 'Women have incredible will-power. I've treated women riddled with parasitic infections, so weak they have to drag themselves to the dispensary with their babies still on their backs. Anaemia makes their faces swell up. Their blood's as thin as water. They always say that they can't die because then there wouldn't be anyone to look after the children. Sometimes, in some places, when a labour is difficult the woman's family believes that the pregnancy must be the result of adultery. She must have done something wrong. You pray that the baby won't be born dead because that would only confirm their suspicions. You guide the baby through the

181

birth-canal, hoping that the uterus won't contract around the child's body. It's always draining.'

'But when everything goes well – aren't you over the moon? Don't you feel a huge satisfaction?'

'I used to. But I've seen a lot of dreadful things. I'd like a break from it. You have to give so much care and attention. For ten years·I've never thought about it; I just did it. I almost considered my job to be sacramental. I have witnessed birth and baptisms and weddings and death without the benefit of irony . . . You attend to other people's life-and-death dramas and then you move on. I've always breathed a sigh of relief at the moving on part. Look at that child. Isn't he an angel?'

A beautiful little boy wrapped in a white woollen *serape* was looking with longing at a display of miniature plastic cars. Suddenly Drusilla stood up and walked over to the boy. She pressed money into his hand and whispered in his ear. When she returned to the table, she and Nerida watched the boy buy several of the cars. Other children rushed at Drusilla but she waved them away.

'That was very generous,' said Nerida.

'It was nothing at all. I can afford it. Look, that boy's happy now. It doesn't take much.'

Alexis was hunkered down in the Superpollo *cantiña* playing scissors-stone-paper while slugging something infernal which had once, before fermentation, been swaying gracefully in a field. While looking dark and desperate enough to blend in, he conversed with alcoholically assisted fluency in Tzotzil. Panamanian salsa blared from a bakelite radio behind the bar. Alexis believed that he was not doing enough with his body; wanted to smoke also and perform a haughty, bone-jarring flamenco – sorry, wrong country, *very* wrong, Spain a sensitive issue but not as sensitive as America, they

182

hate that, the way Americans say America meaning North of the Border, but I think I could get away with it stop thinking now or you'll get a glimpse of yourself here in this moment with this drink in your hand. But he continued to kill the mescal, because it earned him respect in the bar. His crazy stare matched that of his spirit-infested companions. Eugene, on the other hand, was folded up in a corner with his head filed between his hands.

In the evening Alexis returned to the *casa* and hung over the typewriter, the picture of scholarly application, in other words, a barrier, which even Nerida did not try to assail because she did not see that there was a barrier. Outwardly, the desk was occupied by the genuine Dr Alexis Serafin.

Nerida had begun to drive regularly and restlessly to San Cristóbal in order to break up the expanses of time spent rattling around Toos's house. After parking the car near the market, she would visit hardware stores and churches, shops specialising in frothy First Holy Communion dresses, and shrines in the foothills surrounding the town, where supplicants honoured the angels, the saints and Our Lady of Guadalupe, a dark-skinned Virgin frequently enhanced by false eyelashes. These excursions were designed to fill Nerida's memory with exotic and novel images which were stored away for future use, like pre-nuptial linen in a glory box.

On a quiet street off Avenida Vicente Guerrero, she fell in behind a pair of Zinacantecos. Fat cerise woollen tassels dangling from chequered neckerchiefs bobbed against their backs. She wondered how many curious sights and sounds she would have to absorb before she was struck by a revelation. The sun glanced off a brass plaque on a colonial building the colour of parchment. Pausing before the weathered double doors, Nerida saw that she was in the presence of the Centro de Investigaciones Etnográficas.

The doors were framed by slender columns which projected from a background of rusticated masonry. Above the portal a balcony, flanked by conquistador figures, hung over the street. Nerida liked balconies; they suggested to her a combination of reticence and omnipotence. Pushing the door open, she stepped over the sill into a shadowy ante-room, its flaking walls a dim burnt orange. An ornate desk, a telephone and a metal filing cabinet indicated a reception area, but there was no one there to receive her.

She passed into the adjoining room, also unoccupied, which opened on to an arcade and a courtyard. A bark of laughter sounded from the far end of the arcade. Until this moment, Nerida had not expected to find Alexis here, or Eugene. Having heard nothing from them, she had assumed they were still in Xul Vo. Breaching the open door she saw Eugene and four Zinacanteco men, the oldest of whom was grinning to himself at a private joke, all of them sitting around a long table. Eugene was shuffling through a pile of white cards, but his gaze was on the men who were writing slowly. Alexis leant against the wall next to a shelf that held the tape recorder. Its spools revolved lazily. One of the Zinacantecos chuckled and was about to speak, when Eugene glanced up from his index cards and noticed Nerida. She caused a silence.

The Zinacantecos laid down their pens, regarding Nerida impassively. Eugene frowned. Nerida had dressed carefully in order not to offend the local inhabitants, and although soberly attired in an enveloping dress, with her inflammatory blonde hair tucked under a headscarf, she was aware that nothing could disguise the fact that she was a woman, whose gender, judging from Eugene's agitated expression, would sabotage this enquiry.

'Excuse me,' she murmured.

'Nerida,' Alexis exclaimed, 'what a pleasant surprise.'

Eugene nodded stiffly, his cold eyes communicating his

displeasure at the interruption. With one hand on Nerida's shoulder, Alexis led her from the chilly room.

Out in the street she said, 'Sorry. Eugene's furious.'

'He often is. Still, he's got his Ph.D. to fall back on.'

Nerida threaded her hand through the crook of his arm and they swung towards Plaza Central.

Sun slanted into the long narrow dining room of the Hotel Santa Clara, choosing random tables for illumination, including the one occupied by Alexis and Nerida. Alexis sat with his back to a window, unconscious of the halation which fluorescently outlined his head and upper body as if he were imposed on the background as a special effect. The energetic conversations of mestizo businessmen, amplified by ceramic floor-tiles, washed around the room, causing Nerida and Alexis to lean into one another's space. Fluid sentences concerning iguanas, the suppleness of Nerida's hands and a tragi-comic history of the conquistador Don Diego de Mazariego, whose sixteenth-century house formed the nucleus of the hotel, scrolled out of Alexis's mouth and wrapped themselves warmly around Nerida. She responded with the kind of girl-smiles and low-voiced interjections that are chemically equivalent to the bonding elements in powerful adhesives; but after the soup course, she knew that they were not working. Her surface could not stick to Alexis's surface because he would not stay still. The non-verbal Alexis was doing everything much too fast. His eyes flicked around the room, his fingers tapped the rim of his glass, he was churning through the tequila. He was doing everything quickly and nervily except eating. His plate remained untouched.

'Are you getting something out of this work with Eugene?' Nerida asked.

'Yes, I am. It's very fruitful.'

'But he irritates you, doesn't he?'

'Sometimes. It doesn't mean anything. We've always

185

been like that.' He smiled at her, which raised her spirits. 'You know, he doesn't even seem to notice how bleak the Zinacantecos are. How dark and depressed. They're pathological about drink and sex.'

'That's because Eugene romanticises the hard life. I can understand that. He wants to be an *hombre* . . .'

'Don't we all?'

'. . . and then he can forgive himself for coming from El Norte.'

'It's the ethnographer's dilemma. Losing sight of the role you're playing. That interests me,' Alexis stated mildly in order to screen the fact that it obsessed him. Alexis had learned that communication with the Earth Lord, or rather, the double-dealing of anthropology, was a two-edged sword. A clever man might enter his cave and find wealth and happiness, but one wrong step, one lapse in cleverness, and the Earth Lord would imprison his victim in a pair of iron sandals. He could never leave until they had worn out. People were desperate to believe in things that were endless and blue and mythological.

He kissed the air in front of Nerida's face. 'What is it?'

'You've gone interior. You look like you're mentally stealing through the night like some kind of commando, carrying ropes and a grappling-iron. I've been left behind to throw a few tortillas together.'

'I'd never leave you behind.'

Nerida brushed her fingers over his forearm. 'I think my talent for travel is diminishing. How long are we going to stay here?'

'I have to finish these field-notes.'

'What are they for? Are they something to do with Zeugen?'

'Zeugen.' Alexis dribbled the last of the tequila into his mouth. 'That strikes me now as terrifically vicarious.' Taking

186

a deep breath, he buttoned his jacket and combed his hair with his fingers. 'A life spent writing about a life . . .'

The scarlet macaws in the courtyard aviary began to screech at a painful pitch. Their cries diverted Alexis from the conversation. He was looking around for a waiter. Nerida watched a young Indian woman creeping through the restaurant, begging for left-over bread rolls. Waved away by the plump businessmen who were downing cups of coffee, she darted deeper into the dining room until she reached the table at which Nerida and Alexis sat. They recognised Xunka. Xunka flashed an imploring smile at Alexis, but their waiter loomed and in an arm-whirling display of hierarchy, ordered her from the restaurant. She ducked, although he had not aimed a blow at her, and slunk towards the door. Removing money from the table, the waiter clucked disapprovingly. Nerida suddenly seized the rolls, fleetingly aware of Alexis's quizzical expression, and ran after Xunka.

She was loitering in the foyer behind a potted yucca, but as Nerida appeared, clutching the bread rolls to her chest, Xunka bolted from the hotel. Nerida sped out the door into the plaza, calling, 'Xunka! *Por favor!*'

Passersby turned their heads and slowed down. Xunka halted, hunching her shoulders to make herself small and insignificant. Nerida offered the bread with a foolish smile, knowing she had completely overplayed the gesture of generosity. Staring at the ground, Xunka made a hammock of her *rebozo* into which Nerida deposited the rolls. Xunka bundled them up and disappeared.

Alexis was waiting on the hotel steps. Nerida busied herself, brushing crumbs from her dress, then offered him a slightly defiant smile. But he was gazing over her head, scanning the plaza.

21

Exhilarated by the success of their lightning textile-raid, Toos and Drusilla returned triumphantly to the house as night was falling. They were accompanied by a fine-boned woman dressed in a tight serge suit of racing green, her black hair immaculately chignoned. Nerida, who was dissuading Raúl from his ambition to abase himself by polishing, again, every single pair of her shoes, was relieved at their arrival.

Toos, with loving, child-denied arms outstretched, cried, 'Neridita! May I present Juana Cruz Hernández! We discovered her accidentally on the street. She is my old friend, here to see Rafael's mother' – Juana elegantly see-sawed a gloved hand in the air to show that the mother of Rafael was a trial – 'and I bring her to the *casa* for an excellent supper. This is so nice! Where are they? Alexis and Eugene? Surely not still making investigations?'

Alexis and Eugene were propelled from the rooms where they were pursuing their respective, secret labours and intermingled in the *sala*, which was warm and glinting with table-settings, invisibly art-directed by Graciela, and leaping firelight. While also displaying the portable pieces of Guatemala that she and Drusilla had rescued from financially compromised villages, Toos orchestrated introductions. Juana Cruz Hernández had once lived in San Cristóbal, but after having separated from her painter husband Rafael, she had returned to her family in Mexico City. Nerida, enjoying the wry expression sustained by Juana during Toos's no-detail-spared explanation of the failed marriage, learned that Juana taught film at the university in Mexico City and that her mother was part-Indian, from Comitán. Juana, after smiling fondly at Toos, turned to Nerida and said, 'This Toos is a fantastic sweep of a woman, yes? *¡La mujer estoica!*'

Between the appetisers and the main course, an epoch passed during which Eugene fumbled a story from Xul Vo involving silver-heeled demons, shotguns and a virgin. Juana, while listening politely, was paying attention to Nerida and Alexis, noting the fraying, but replaceable bonds. Eugene digressed to explain how he had extracted the tale from his informants. His smile stretched like a rubber band at breaking point as the telling wore on. Realisation of the chasm between his own narrative expertise and that of his sources was written on his despairing face. Nerida felt a lurch of sympathy for him.

Alexis interrupted, his voice slicing neatly through Eugene's story. 'The last time we were at Xul Vo, Eugene advertised himself as the assiduous field-worker. But the whole point of the exercise – come on, Gene, admit it – was to catch a glimpse of beautiful, bad Xunka. I think you have visions of marrying her and settling down to an authentic Zinacanteco life.'

Eugene flushed, embarrassed. Juana, cocking an eyebrow in Alexis's direction, asked, 'You too are an anthropologist? You work with Eugene?'

'I do. Our excursions are vital to my study of impotence. The affectional kind, of course.'

Eugene looked round at the others, with an aggrieved expression. Nerida and Toos began to fold napkins and replace the tops of condiments and wipe their hands of crumbs in an automatic impulse to order and soothe. Eugene decided to be magnanimous. 'Say what you like. It doesn't bother me.'

Alexis laughed. 'I talk about myself here, Gene. I'm talking about love. Love turned bourgeois is – it makes you walk up and down in a restless stupor.' Eugene became mesmerised by a dried-flower arrangement on the sideboard. Alexis felt confused by a rage that was concentrating itself in an unspoken condemnation of Eugene's shirt . . . I hate his shirt. That denim shirt with the sweat stains under the arms . . . and then, with a spasm of despair, was turned on himself. I wake in the night repeating 'zayin, zayin'. Zed. A weapon. My vanity is a large lake and a woman rises holding a sword, but I am too busy admiring my reflection to notice. I fear these images. People ought to be protected from me.

Alexis added, 'You long for something to intervene. You long to risk something and then violence and the threat of disgrace seem attractive.'

Nerida felt a flicker of panic.

'As you can tell,' Drusilla addressed Juana, 'Alexis is not so much an anthropologist as a devolving linguist.'

Juana turned to Nerida while she was waiting for Alexis to don his jacket – he had made up for his unmannerly lapse at the dinner table by offering to drive Juana back to town – and said, 'Would you like my address, Nerida? You may have some reason to visit Mexico City in the future.'

'Thank you, I'd like to see you again.'

'Fantastic. You turn up on my doorstep – any time.'

'Like fate, with a bouquet of roses.'

'Yes. Like fate. You can never tell how she will look.'

Tearing a page from a notebook, Juana wrote out her address in a loopy hand and passed the paper to Nerida. She patted Nerida's hand with warm, dry fingers. 'I wish I could stay longer,' she said, 'but I have left my son with my sister and I am anxious to see him. Toos said to me that you are a photographer but we have had no opportunity, I regret, to speak about that.'

'Yes, I am.'

'Rafael was forever destroying his canvases. He would paint and paint and become furious because he did not see a masterpiece there. What do you make of that?'

'I don't know. A fantasy of omnipotence?'

'I think so. I think that exactly.'

'How old is your son?'

'Six. I adore him. I bring him back here on his birthdays so that he knows where he is from.'

When Juana and Alexis had left, Nerida stood at the french doors drinking a second, superfluous cup of coffee. She could see Eugene reflected in the night-affected glass. He punched a cushion into shape on the sofa and then changed his mind about sitting down. Seeking to preempt a complaint about Alexis's behaviour, Nerida strolled towards the hearth and said, 'What happened to Xunka? She's back in her village? I gave her some bread rolls the other day.'

Eugene sat down suddenly. 'She was here?'

'No. I saw her at the Santa Clara.'

Eugene tsk-tsked. 'There's no need for that. She could work here.'

'I don't think she and Graciela see eye to eye. There was an argument about the laundry.'

'Someone should have told me. I would have made her see sense. There's no one to stand up for her.'

'Can't she stand up for herself?'

'You have no idea. You don't know what it's like for Xunka.'

'What is it like?'

'She has no one to protect her. Her family's pretty far gone. Her father's dead now but he always drank too much. Xunka had a suitor, I think he was called Xun. But she ran

191

away from him. They hauled her into court to make her see her obligation. The *presidente* told her to choose Xun, but she wouldn't. That's kind of extreme for a Zinacanteca. Her parents had to pay back the money Xun spent courting her. Her brothers were pretty riled about it, especially Petul the oldest one. He's a maniac, always picking fights.'

'So she's gone back to her family?'

'I don't see how she can.' Eugene's next question surprised Nerida. 'What happened with Lexie in London? I heard from Francis Lipton.'

'What did you hear?'

'Well. General flakiness. Francis was worried.'

'Alexis was ill, that's why we left.'

Eugene nodded and waited, expecting more. He regarded Nerida with the faintest shadow of a smile on his face. 'Uh-huh. I'm worried about Alexis, too. I hope you don't mind my saying this – and you know I've always regarded him as a kind of mentor – but I get the feeling he's going a little bit off the rails. He's not contributing.'

'Then you should speak to him about it.'

'It's a delicate subject. I'd say it required a woman's touch.'

Eugene rose to his feet and for the second time that evening, Nerida's hand was patted, only this time the touch was ambiguous. 'Let's sleep on it. I'm sure you'll figure out what to do.' He made a number of minor adjustments to his clothes, then added as he strolled towards the stairs, 'It must be driving you crazy having nothing to do.'

Nerida placed her empty coffee cup on the mantel, then, quelling the assumption that someone, a servant, would pick up after her, returned it to the silent kitchen, rinsed the cup and saucer and placed them in the wooden drainer. During her absence, someone had extinguished all the lights in the *sala*. Walking the length of the shadowy room, observing tonal relationships, a white chair had become silver, a blue curtain was now smoky, Nerida felt as sensitive as a photographic emulsion, whose particles of silver halide were about to be activated by exposure to light. With difficulty she undid the bolts on the doors and strolled into the courtyard where she inhaled the antiseptic night air which smelled of pine. A full moon hung heavily in the sky. Nerida cast her mind back to a time when Hippocrates was still alive, trying to separate medicine from superstition. People without electricity are much more aware of moonlight. They believed that the frequency of seizures varied with the moon phase. On moonless nights, the darkness was filled with ordinary, acceptable fears, the fear of wild animals on the prowl or other marauders; but that was preferable to lunacy. You have to be a pretty colossus of a woman to tumble conceit. One of those massive goddesses wearing a marble chiton. You have to be pretty enormous, bordering on mythological, to burst the shackles that you yourself have begged for.

You love someone to overcome desolation of the soul, although not everyone is convinced by that imperative.

You fall sleep. Then you wake up.

For five weeks, while Alexis was working a fervid schedule as Eugene's shadow, Nerida took her camera everywhere – except to Xul Vo or San Cristóbal. Toos, making no comment for once, arranged to have more film stock couriered via Juana from Mexico City. Drusilla, too, was silenced by Nerida's activity, because Nerida was not available to play. There had been no blinding moment, as Nerida had once anticipated, in which she had been anointed by inspiration. It had happened by increments. Waking in the night, alone, thinking: Where is Alexis? Thinking: I am jealous of Drusilla and that is her intent. I think Eugene is useless and that is not my problem. I have run out of clothes and make-up and rationalisations. You can spend six-figure amounts of time, you can go way over your credit limit, which is your whole life, in fact, trying to figure out the motives and meaning behind your fellow travellers' behaviour and all it adds up to is an anecdotal colourful history, low on personal satisfaction. Nerida had always wanted to travel and become multi-layered and multi-faceted by virtue of observation and revel in lovely passivity; carried through historical streets on a litter, occasionally snapping a picture so she could say that she'd been there. But now, in the middle of the night in a foreign country, her eyes opened and she thought: How weak, how retarded. How about simply pressing the trigger?

Nerida rose one morning, loaded the camera into the Dodge and found her subject, even if it did escape close questioning, occurring all over the rugged, latent landscape. The Earth Lord. The cross shrine. Five sacred mountains. Making tortillas. Wedding at dawn. Face of the maize. Shaman prays for a patient. She fixed her camera to the tripod and began to shoot, discovering in the process that she had a gift for exposure latitude, acutance, the law of reciprocity, characteristic curves and most of all, the emotion that transcends equipment.

She went about her work quietly. No need to make a hue and cry, to hoist banners bearing your personal monogram. It's an effective disguise: pretty girl with camera, which lets her enter territories suspicious of men wearing hand-beaten academic armour. He who tries too hard to be significant finds himself becoming dead beat. A burst balloon. A rag.

She tore up magazines. When she had found the images she wanted – fragments of mountain, desert, rain cloud; examples of whiteware and eyewear; variations of the colour blue: ultramarine, cobalt, indigo, Antwerp and Prussian – she locked the camera into position, then released the single-frame lever at different rates, animating the cut-outs, directed by the accumulation of thousands of observations and sensations which had seemed insubstantial at the time. She had no idea what she would do with the footage, but this did not disturb her. She was not thinking of the applause. The idea of posterity was redundant because it was always in the future and, she believed, if you thought about it in the here-and-now, it clogged up the moment.

To her surprise she suffered little rejection in the hamlets, because she struck those she filmed as neither an anthropologist nor a tourist, and while undeniably an outsider, she had found that offering money was effective. Especially in the run-up to the Christmas-New Year fiesta frenzy when there were so many costumes to make and chickens to buy. A period of intense ritual was approaching Zinacantan in a year already soaked in ceremony. Ten days before Christmas celebrating the Virgen de Navidad. Flower renewal. Cargo exchange. The beating of turtle-shell drums. Dance dramas. A bull kills a few masked husbands. Unmasked wives lift their skirts. Symbolic angels plunge symbolic knives into the body of the symbolic bull. Graciela constructs turkey in *mole poblano* for Christmas Day. Nerida did not concern herself with questions of soul-stealing or invasions of privacy because in the past she, too, had been paid to be photographed.

On a pallet somewhere or in a hammock, and occasionally in his bed at the *casa* with Nerida lying naked but in oceanic, satisfied sleep beside him, Alexis, feeling hot and distraught, remained awake. A long time ago he had cut a dash in continental streets. He was trying to remember how to be charming; but he had misplaced that aspect of himself. Without Drusilla's encouragement he might have given up and retreated to the ordinary world. Much later he thought about those last few days

195

in Zinacantan and was stunned at how completely he had shut his eyes and his ears to all the signs around him which, like screaming sirens and flashing red lights, illustrated an emergency.

22

In January, when the imminent fiesta of San Sebastian pre-occupied all of Zinacantan, Nerida laid down her camera. Stored in London were cartons of neatly ordered negatives and carefully written accounts of her experiments with speed and light at the film-makers' co-operative. As she recorded details of the footage she had shot in and around the hamlets, she measured her present gratifying sense of achievement against the past where a holographic Nerida could be glimpsed, looking almost lifelike, aimlessly alphabetising and ordering by date and location. A prevaricating Nerida who had kept all her material in abeyance.

To exercise her legs, which were stiff from the two hours spent crouching on the floor sorting the film canisters, Nerida set off for the hill behind the house. As she strode through the arch, she saw Drusilla doubled over the lip of the well, reaching into its depths. She was motionless but there was a tension about her body that made Nerida wonder if she was considering throwing herself in.

'Drusilla!'

Drusilla's head moved slightly, but she did not look up. When Nerida reached the well she saw that Drusilla's hands gripped the thin wrists of a child. He hung above the black water, his eyes wide and glazed. He whimpered. There was hardly room for both of the women to reach into the narrow

197

shaft, but Drusilla did not have the strength to haul the child up alone.

'Take his left hand,' she whispered.

The dangling child sobbed as Nerida closed her hand over his forearm. Together the women hauled him up, until he collapsed over the stone kerb and tumbled to the ground. Drusilla, making soothing sounds, tried to examine his grazed limbs, but he pushed her away, scrambled to his feet and ran from them.

'How did he get in there?'

'I've no idea. I came out to pick lemons and heard him crying. He was hanging on to the edge. I started to pull him out and he panicked. His hands were muddy and he fell back down. Then I couldn't get enough leverage to pull him up by myself. He might have drowned.'

They placed the cover over the well, anchored it with a rock and began to walk back to the house. Their shared rescue of the boy made Nerida believe that she and Drusilla had drawn, momentarily, closer together.

'Thank you,' said Drusilla. 'I'm so glad you were here. Are you giving your camera a rest?'

'Yes, I am. I've done all I can.'

'Why don't you go to Mexico City for a while? You must be dying to look at your stuff on a screen.'

'That's exactly what I'd like to do. I'm going to suggest it to Alexis. I think it's time we left.'

Drusilla frowned at her dirty hands. 'Since you're free now, why don't we go for a drive? Just as soon as I've cleaned myself up.'

Sitting compactly at the wheel of the Dodge, Drusilla drove up a steep, tyre-shredding road. A couple of trolleys, wooden bases on pram wheels, steered by ropes, appeared on the crest of the hill. They were piloted by withered Zinacanteco men. The trolleys swerved violently to avoid the Dodge and were in danger of losing their teetering cargo of firewood, but recovering, they whipped down the incline. Nerida and Drusilla continued into the evergreen cloud forest where mosses and epiphytes had colonised the trees.

They stopped at a clearing adjacent to the road, where they unwrapped chicken tacos and uncapped bottles of soft drink. Nerida shivered. Drusilla glided to the car and returned with a sweater which she handed over, wordlessly. Nerida slid her arms and her face through the perfumed cashmere apertures, then watched Drusilla eat. She took tiny bites from the overstuffed taco and yet somehow consumed it at great speed.

Without looking at Nerida, Drusilla said in an offhand way, 'You think Alexis is out of character at the moment. But that's the real Alexis. He's afflicted.' A dog barked in the forest and then they heard children laughing. Drusilla flung the remains of her taco at the trees. 'He had some fits when he was thirteen, at school. Did he tell you that?'

'Not specifically.'

'Despite his superficial mastery of everything on the curriculum, he's always been flawed. I know because I looked after him. After the fits he was brought home for tests. The results were fine, but when we were home from school the following summer, I noticed that he still suffered from absences. They usually occurred in the morning. They only lasted perhaps twenty or thirty seconds each one, so no one else was aware of them. He didn't want anyone else to know. In the middle of playing or reading he would suddenly be still, quite blank, then do this thing of stroking his eyebrow. It was hard for him. He was under our father's thumb. He always had to be luminous.'

'I know.'

Drusilla's face said: I don't think so. 'Once Alexis was writing. Suddenly he grabbed another sheet of paper and scribbled furiously on it and then ran to me with the paper held out in front of him. It said: "Got no speak" in mirror writing. Later he tried to write like that and couldn't.'

'What about you?'

'I saw through Papa very early on. After that he avoided the connection. My mother taught me everything I know about dressing well and creating an atmosphere. I'm not being tart. It's a considerable skill.'

'I agree. I learnt that lesson myself. But you also had the advantage of education.'

'My father never taught us Czech, you know. It's odd to hear your parents speaking in a language you don't understand. It sounded like English played backwards.'

A dog limped into their clearing. A discharge leaked from one of its red eyes. Two children were visible now, staring through the trees at the foreign women. They were small, black-haired children wearing woollen tunics and straw hats. One of them whistled and the dog, resigned, stumbled back in their direction.

Nerida said, 'I've got this strong feeling that something bad is going to happen to Alexis if we stay here. Something worse than epilepsy.'

'Why don't you stop fretting? You can see that he's working. Besides, I'm enjoying his company. We were separated for a long time.'

Nerida thought to herself that childhood could be a very dreary, unnecessary prison. 'You can visit us in another place.'

'Where?'

'Anywhere. There's the whole world. Somewhere semi-permanent. I'm not as restless as I was.'

'Be realistic, Nerida. There's nowhere for Alexis to go. He'll never get a decent post again. Do you realise that if I hadn't stopped him he would have stolen Constantin's work?

That's how desperate he is. And everyone knows about it. We are here because it's his refuge.'

It angered Nerida to hear Alexis spoken of as powerless and wrecked. She didn't care what had happened between him and Constantin as long as he did not end up in the same featureless no man's land as his doomed colleague, escorted there on a stretcher by Drusilla, the senior medical officer.

'Drusilla – were you in love with Constantin?' Did you love him as remorselessly as you love Alexis?

Drusilla threw Nerida a very dry look and began shoving their picnic debris into a plastic bag. She scrunched up the bag and brushed pine needles from her skirt. 'How could I love someone who was so bent on destroying himself?'

'Because you specialise in rescue and repair. Those are your conditions for loving someone.'

Drusilla laughed. 'Of course I rescue and repair. But only medically.'

'Only in every way you can think of! Let Alexis go. He's sick and it's nothing you can fix. He will cure himself. He has to.'

Drusilla turned her head away so that Nerida's words were deflected. She looked at her watch and said calmly, 'Toos is having an opening at the gallery at four. She's expecting a lot of rich Americans who are here for the fiesta. You can keep the sweater on. It'll be cold by the time we get there.'

As they hurtled around the treacherous bends of the mountain road, Nerida could not figure out why Drusilla was so unenraged by Nerida's attack. She was as opaque as the sacrificial well at Chichén Itzá where gold and turquoise offerings had once languished in the sediment among skulls, fragments of bone and scraps of carbonised cloth. But it didn't matter. Nerida felt lively and purposeful because in a matter of days she and Alexis would be flying across the border. She thought of asking Drusilla to drop her off now

201

at the *casa* so that Nerida could put her arms around Alexis and speak truthfully. Drusilla, however, had already turned on to the road leading to San Cristóbal. Serenely, she drove Nerida away from the house.

Shall I stop being a dead person? A spook?

In the *casa*, Alexis sat at his desk, possessed by false certainties. He was convinced that all the years he had spent studying the life of Samuel Zeugen had been in vain. There was no point in writing a commentary that could only ever be second-hand, second-guessing, second-rate. He had come to believe that scholarship was a very leukaemic occupation. It thinned the blood and withered the brain. He, in contrast, was fabricating a manifesto of confessional double-dealing which featured himself as the fateful agent. The object of his existence was to implement all his incessant knowledge in a stealthy work of art: a searing version of Eugene Rinehart, ethnographer, his theory and practice, in which Eugene was obliterated by the true subject – Alexis. The second, but infinitely more artful, Dr Serafin.

Alexis drove his pen over the page, his thoughts too urgent to type. I will not be secondary. I desire to be the first person. I. I. I. The Old Phoenician sign of Z, which has always been my one and true fetish, the key to gratification. It opens a door to the past where the chain of creativity lies unbroken. A long time ago I generated electromagnetism. Then around 3,000 BC, the eschatologically minded Egyptians drew an arrow and aimed it at my future. It tore through time, accruing identity. About 1,500 BC, the Semites in Syria and Palestine modified the arrow, calling it zayin, a weapon, before relaunching it. Engraved with the name of Zeus, it lodged in an empty space, the sixth space, in the Greek alphabets, in the green alphabet of the Dorian Islands and the dark-blue alphabet of the west coast of Asia Minor, in the Phrygian and Lycian and Lydian alphabets where the letter transformed itself into zeta, but it remained a weapon. The letter zoomed on, ripped out of the Greek alphabet by pragmatic Romans who attached it to the end of theirs in order to show that it was strange.

After a blur of centuries, it invaded my childhood.

'Want to play a game, Alexis?'

Drusilla sat opposite him and handed him a card on which she had written in a precociously assured hand:

L M F K J P A W X Y Z 5 6
O X O X O X O X O X O O O

'I can't remember how to play.'

'You mean you've never known how to play. How could you? I made it up. It's my game.'

'You know everything, Dru.'

'You have to guess what goes to what and where the arrow goes. If you guess wrongly it's my turn and so on until all the letters are used up and all the letters are connected.'

Alexis wanted to please her as he wanted to please his parents. Even the apprehension that he was about to be humiliated did not deter him from embarking on an amusement of which he had no understanding.

'You go first.'

'I can't start unless you guess. It doesn't work otherwise. Which letter do you choose?'

Alexis pointed at a J.

'So what does it connect with?'

'K?'

'Wrong! J connects with F. It was staring you in the face.'

With a red felt pen, Drusilla drew a confident arrow from J to F. 'F is for Fiona, of course.' This was the name of their neighbour's twelve-year-old daughter who was the same age

203

as Drusilla. 'And Fiona's little brother is called Jonathan. So there is also the connection between sisters and brothers. Do you see that?'

Alexis could not grasp the connection rationally, but there were many oblique things he did not yet understand. 'Your turn to guess. What goes with P?'

'X.'

'X?'

'Because X is spiky. Therefore it needs to be with a letter that has a little curve. You know that J has already been used up, leaving only a P.'

Alexis drew an arrow from P to X. The line wobbled. 'What about five and six? They've got curves. And all the zeros.'

'You lunatic. Those are *numbers*! Go on, guess again. Connect M with which letter?'

'Could it be L?'

'Very good. Because?'

'Because they're next to one another.'

'Aha! You've fallen into the trap of thinking that it's because they're next to one another.' Drusilla leashed M to L with a red line. 'L and M go together because if they had an E, an O and an N, they would spell "LEMON".'

'Oh.'

They played on. Alexis made wild guesses which were sometimes incinerated on the pyre of Drusilla's perplexing logic, while others senselessly struck home.

'What does Z go with, Dru?'

'Five and six.'

'Can you explain?'

'You're going to have to learn to work this out for yourself some day, Alexis. Z looks almost like a five and six looks almost like a five so they belong together.'

'It doesn't look much like a five to me.'

'It does if you look at it from my point of view. Also, there are the noughts.'

'You said they were zeros.'

'Now I'm calling them noughts. I'm in charge of this game and so I can call them anything I want. I'm the one who has to make sense of it. Here we have nought, cross, nought, cross, nought, cross, nought, cross, nought, cross, which is five pairs. Then you reach Z which is above a nought.'

Alexis's head hurt. The kind of sinus-pain that struck you in a high, cold wind that cut across a rugby ground on a Saturday morning, while you were stamping your feet on the side-lines, designated a subsitute.

Drusilla leaned in close to secure his concentration. 'You move on to five and find to your surprise that the cross you have been expecting has turned into a nought. And again, under six, there is another nought.'

With a stab of excitement, Alexis felt himself enter Drusilla's mode of thought. 'Because they're all under the influence of Z?'

'Yes! And because they are under the influence of Z we can now, finally, call these last three noughts zeros. Do you understand? Z goes with two things, which is more than any other letter, but it also governs zero zero which is less than any other letter. The person who guesses where Z goes wins the game.' Drusilla gazed at him pityingly. 'I'm afraid you didn't win.'

Alexis wanted to win more than anything in the world. He stared at the Z, trying to quell the sob rising in his constricted throat. To comfort him Drusilla allowed him to lie down with his head in her lap. Stroking his hair, she murmured, 'Little doll. Pretend you're my baby.'

Snuggling into her lap, he drew his knees up foetally, which made him pleasantly smaller, and wrapped his arms tightly around her. There was so much to learn in the world.

'Baby, baby, baby. Kiss Mama.' She bent her head so he could kiss her mouth. After a minute, Drusilla said briskly, 'Now you're grown up. Try to kill me.'

She stretched out on the floor. Kneeling with his skinny legs on either side of her hips, Alexis raised his arm, clutching an imaginary dagger. With all his strength he drove his dagger at her but she clamped her hand around his wrist and resisted him. She was unyielding. He pushed as hard as he could, both of them breathing heavily with the effort, their eyes locked on one another hypnotically. No matter how he pressed, he could not make her defer. She was much stronger than he. Exhausted, he collapsed and rolled on to his back. They lay side by side, happy. Each made up to the other for the absence of their parents.

After a while Drusilla whispered, 'Do you want to play again?'

'The Z game?'

'No, the murdering one.'

It must have been then that the two games merged, long ago.

The letter Z is always divisive, schizophrenic, and martial. After the successful strike on Pearl Harbour, Admiral Yamamoto raised the signal Z, as he had in 1905 to claim victory in the Russo-Japanese war.

The letter Z is grand. Its voice is declamatory, accompanied by thunder and lightning. It is louder than love.

The letter Z springs from tension. As the 'zero' person, linguistically, the unmarked term, it forms one of the central oppositions among grammatical categories, that opposition between the speaking subject and the forms of the third person, between lyric poetry as the poetry of the first person, and epic poetry as the poetry of the third. Zeugen. *NarZiss*.

On the subject of pools, do not lean over too far to look at your reflection. Only Tezcatipoca, the Jaguar god, can look with impunity into this mirror. That is how he discovers what is in the hearts and minds of men.

Alexis's hand hovered. Then he pressed his nib hard into the soft paper . . . and it's saying: 'Unzipped gaze. Quizzical mestizo. Blazing schizophrenic. Rendezvous in the *zócalo*. Zinacanteca. Zinacanteca . . .'

Now in the space of nothing he saw a hole in his narrative. It was the size of the Sumidero canyon where Indians had jumped to their deaths rather than be captured by *conquistadors*. It was the size of a university campus. It was the missing climax. He lacked the juice of risk.

His mouth had turned into the Sahara. He wandered into the kitchen and gulped a large tumbler of water, but still remained thirsty. Nothing would happen if he stayed in the house. He felt compelled to leave the domesticated interior. The house represented confined thought. The landscape represented action.

Alexis closed the front door behind him. He wanted to walk round in circles like those hawks out there in the sky, shadowy things swooping and dipping. Instead he got into the Volkswagen. The sky was so white he couldn't look into it. He drove his car on a road laid out by an anarchist, looking for a collision. When a photon collides with an atom, the electron is hurled into a transcendent orbit. Simultaneously the electron is both there and here. It was cold here in Calvinist Southland. Tussock grew on the shoulders of the road, while the fields beyond appeared to be covered with snow. But Nerida, she had grown up in hot and fecund Northland, where the insurgent inhabitants of mixed blood sat on sagging porches and did not care about the state of their architecture.

He climbed out of the car, leaving the door swinging, and walked into a cornfield. A shimmering on the periphery of his vision caused him to raise his hand to shade his eyes.

Flocks of birds in the blinding sky. They meant him harm. Flocks of zeds in the night sky, hovering over him, their claws extended, dying to pick at his brain. He crooked his arms over his head to protect himself, but nevertheless, he was irradiated by the terrible moonlight.

She wandered towards him unconcerned about the darkness above or the creatures. Bats. He told himself they were bats. The rustle of zeds retreated. She had long, thin, black plaits threaded through with ribbons. She didn't know how to kiss. She ran her tongue over his lips. As she fell down at his feet, neither he nor she noticed the children spying on them from behind the trees. She spoke Tzotzil, a foreign language. Xunka. She spoke the language of catastrophe.

23

On the morning of the first day of the fiesta of San Sebastián, Alexis opened his eyes in darkness, having woken, sweating from excremental dreams. The weighty curtains in the bedroom admitted a sliver of moonlight, which bounced off the mirror on the dresser so that the glass gleamed bleakly. Nerida was curled up in the bed, close to the wall. To stabilise himself, he placed his hand on her head. Nothing happened. No current was transmitted. Hooking his forearm around her neck, he dragged her towards him. She made a confused sound, so he covered her mouth with one hand. With the other he searched between her legs for something sweet. She was moving restlessly beneath him but he would not take his hand from her mouth. When he tried to enter her, his cock refused. For some time he struggled, but he could not achieve any pleasure. As the sun rose, inserting a beam of light into the bedroom, Alexis said, as casually as he could, that on account of an inexplicable nausea, he would not go to the fiesta. Without looking into Nerida's face, he pressed his mouth on her tangled hair and then pulled a pillow over his head and pretended to be asleep until she had left the room.

Then he sat up. He could not remember anything that had happened in the previous twenty-four hours. He told himself that this was not unusual. He had experienced absences before whose sick aftermath was the price he paid for inspiration. In fact he had longed for their return. But never before had he felt cut loose from Nerida. When he had touched her no tremor passed through his fingers. A circuit was broken. As he examined his right hand, an instinctive revulsion made his stomach clench. He implored his memory to explain why he felt like a man who has come home to find his house a smoking ruin and his wife seized by fascists, but no images came to his aid. He was plagued instead by the word '*machete*' from the Spanish '*macho*', which means a hammer and a broad, heavy knife or cutlass. It is used as both a tool and a weapon.

Unaware that his judgement was destroyed, Alexis descended to the room below where he bent over his manuscript in the belief that everything he wrote there was sensible and heartfelt and, therefore, excusable.

Toos surged through the noisy crowd making its way to the church of San Sebastián, her roomy rucksack, with a thinly rolled mat buckled to it, slung over one shoulder. Drusilla and Nerida swung along behind her, enjoying the anticipatory buzz around them. Nerida was determined to enjoy it. She had not been able to communicate with Alexis. Even when she was face to face with him, he didn't seem to be there. In the distance, the land rose gradually, above pastures and other evidence of cultivation, to form a perfectly conical mountain, an old volcano.

Eugene, slightly agitated, was turning his head this way and that. He was searching for someone, other than the three women he had arranged to meet. Then he clapped his hands together. 'Well now. Mass is over. I think we can go in.'

He steered a path for Nerida with one nervous hand at the small of her back. She noticed that they were regarded with stony stares by several Zinacanteco men, and felt a tightening in Eugene's fingers indicating that he had noticed it too.

'Anything you want to know, just ask,' he said staring at the flat sky.

In the south-west corner of the churchyard stood a peculiar dead tree about six or seven metres tall, stripped of its bark. Eugene identified it as the Jaguar Tree. A drum began to beat loudly and the chatty babble of the crowd segued into a cacophony of cheers and shrieks. Nerida craned her neck, trying to see past the head-gear of those around her. Eugene made room, improving her sightline, but she was jammed up against him. Half a dozen creatures, in brown leather trousers and black cotton jackets, their faces smeared with charcoal, bounded, backwards, into the churchyard. In one hand each leaping dancer brandished a stuffed squirrel, in the other he held a pointed stick. The undersides of the dead animals were painted red.

'Black-men,' Drusilla whispered, also pressing herself against Nerida.

Eugene hunched his shoulders, turning side on so that he and Nerida were no longer touching. 'The squirrels are the wives of the officials who have neglected their religious duties. And the dancers in orange coming in now are the Jaguars.'

Two Jaguars capered before them, also carrying stuffed squirrels and sticks, and whips. They panted – huh-huh-huh-huh – like animals in heat. At the appearance of the sacred drum, borne on a tumpline by one man and struck by the percussionist following him, cheers swelled anew. Eugene's face was flushed as if he were intoxicated. A mocking jeer rose from the crowd as several flashy creatures pranced into the yard on horseback.

'Whiteheads!' Eugene yelled over the noise.

Arrayed in white and red, they wore outrageous hats upon their turbans. Light glanced from the mirrors and rosaries hanging around their necks and from the tin-foil decorations on their foreheads. The Whiteheads excited slurs from the crowd, but these were nothing compared to the abuse that greeted the next apparitions – men dressed grotesquely as

211

Spanish ladies. Staying their horses, they displayed themselves to the spectators while daintily raising tiny combs to
their hair. Their long purple veils shimmered. An excess of
mirrors and rosaries dangled from their necks and wrists.
Nerida recognised civilization.

Eugene breathed in her ear, 'Indians know that *ladinos* think
Indians are dirty and lazy. But the Indians think these white
women are an abomination. They're vain and conceited.
They'll sleep with anyone.'

Suddenly, one of the Black-men sprang forward raising
his animal high in the air. A righteous roar answered his
declamation, then the crowd quietened. Tightening his grip
on the sharp stick held in his right hand, the ritualist paused
for effect and then, with a screech, rammed the pike into the
squirrel's stigmatised genitals.

'Aaiiee!' he cried, agitating the stick in a frenzy. He seemed
to be screaming, *yes, yes, yes, yes, yes*!

'What's happening?' Nerida asked, shivering.

'The squirrel thing is kind of the bad wife. This is to show
her she can't just go running wild or everyone will suffer.'

'What's he saying?'

'Something like – she wants to do it anywhere.' He plunged
his hands into his back pockets. 'He buys things, ribbons and
stuff, for his wife instead of giving money to the church.
And . . . this woman . . .' Eugene's voice trailed away as
the other Black-men and Jaguars ferociously impaled their
animals. Their leader renewed his denunciation.

Nerida jogged Eugene's arm. 'What now?'

'More of the same. She wants to climb on top. She'll screw
even in a churchyard.' He patted her shoulder reasssuringly.
'OK, watch this. Here comes the Jaguar.'

The beast prowled up and down, scanning the audience. He
panted, huh-huh-huh, working himself up. Among the circles
on his black-cloth costume, Nerida could make out a jaguar

painted over his heart. Choosing his victim, he pounced, aiming insults at a woman among the spectators directly opposite Nerida's group. Those around the woman shrank away, exposing her more fully to the Jaguar's recriminations. She was dragging her *rebozo* over her face.

'What is it? What has she done?'

'She doesn't even make tortillas. Something something. Fucking bitch.' Eugene smiled apologetically. 'Ah – all she does is spread her legs . . . etcetera.'

Nerida felt alienated. She had stopped enjoying herself. She wanted to fight her way back to Alexis, but she was trapped by bodies.

Cringing, the woman backed slowly away from the Jaguar.

Then the Jaguar, wielding the battered animal, selected a fresh transgressor. But Nerida could not take her eyes off the original victim who was making no effort to reclaim her place or join in the shouting. Shuffling to the perimeter of the yard, the woman lifted her *rebozo* to rearrange its folds. At once Nerida recognised Xunka, inevitable Xunka, and felt exasperated by the woman's endemic ill-fortune. Nerida glanced at Eugene and saw that he was gazing at Xunka with shock on his face.

A demon dressed as a white woman materialised in the yard's entranceway. He nursed a white baby doll. Xunka, her eyes downcast, almost collided with him. He used the doll to swat her away. She fled into the field. Nerida saw that Eugene was scuttling after Xunka, unable to break into a run for fear of drawing attention to himself and the object of his pursuit, but he was observed anyway, balefully, by members of the audience. Once he was out in the field, Eugene came to a standstill. Xunka had disappeared. He looked helplessly around him, then retreated stolidly to the churchyard.

They ate in a scrubby field some distance from the church

within sight of the limestone boulder which was home to the Jaguars. At the base of the boulder stood a shrine marked by three wooden crosses. Eugene said nothing about sighting Xunka so Nerida, too, held her tongue. They praised the stuffed chillies, sweetened squash and juicy *enchiladas* prepared by Graciela, lingering over the food as an increasing number of spectators strolled past them in the direction of the Jaguar Rock, none of them acknowledging Eugene's occasional greetings. Eugene frowned and turned to Toos.

'Why aren't they speaking to me? I don't get it.'

'Did you have a quarrel, a disagreement? You know they will make a theatre of it.'

Eugene shook his head.

Drusilla said, 'Everyone has been drinking. They are not themselves.'

But Nerida believed that the surly response to their presence was nothing to do with alcohol. Somehow they had offended, or at least Eugene had. She could feel his gaze on her. 'What is it?'

'I'm wondering,' Eugene said tensely, 'whether your running around with a camera has upset them. I never thought it was a great idea. I'm not being critical, but it takes years to understand this culture. Maybe you filmed something you shouldn't have – I don't know. Maybe you forced a situation or didn't understand that you should have left. That's not your fault. You don't speak the language. Maybe you made a mistake.'

'Eugene . . . it's possible. Who knows? I could have made someone angry, but if I did I'm sure they would have told me or it would have become known to me then and there. Anyway I paid them straight up, like I used to be paid, and I did a lot of talking, even though I don't speak Tzotzil. I told them everything about myself – '

'How?'

'I showed them pictures. I told them I was far from home and I explained how the camera worked. We shared information about decoration. We sewed sequins. I know how to plait hair and I know what it's like to live in a small place. I made corn fritters. I can sing. I sang plenty of songs. I know a lot about smiling and receding into the background but most of all, I didn't have to do it, if it wasn't going to work out. I wasn't after anything except those beautiful images and when they asked me where the film was going I said, truthfully, to a friend in Mexico City who is from Comitán. It wasn't going to destroy my livelihood or my reputation if I didn't get the shots and that's why I think that none of those hard looks you're getting today has anything to do with me. I'm harmless and they know it.'

Toos began to laugh. 'It's nice you think it's that simple. But you haven't been here very long, Neridita.'

Eugene and Drusilla were smiling too at Nerida's naivety. Toos said, 'It's good you found something to do, but it takes more than your pretty smile. We have been in these places for years and we still step carefully.'

Nerida regarded the implacable trinity ranged opposite her. She saw that Eugene, Drusilla and Toos were united by a need to defeat the efforts of *arrivistes* such as herself, whose failure to penetrate the exotic world improved the status of those who had served their time. Nerida's patience burnt up, leaving among the ashes a huge resistance to this ethnographic, silk-weaving, haunted place of paralysis. While an incantation drifted across the field, she began to think about expirations and conclusions and dusting down suitcases.

She spent most of the next day in her bedroom, writing notes to accompany her eight silent topics. They were more closely connected than she had realised when she had filmed them and it delighted her to discover, after

215

the event, that her subconscious had done so much work for her.

The Earth Lord
Caves, limestone sinks, wells, waterholes. Large white man living underground surrounded by sacks of money and flocks of animals. A woman and a man make love. (Animation.) The Earth Lord sends lightning bolts through their heads.

Wedding at dawn
After a 5 a.m. wedding ceremony at the church of San Lorenzo, the wedding party drinks a bottle of rum outside the church. Many beds (animation) and the bride on them.

Making tortillas
The cycle of making tortillas. Boiling the maize kernels in the lime water to soften them, the night before. The woman awakes before dawn. For two or three hours grinds maize. Pats out tortillas and cooks them. A woman in the kitchen, her skirt raised.

Shaman prays for a patient
A shaman appeals to the ancestral gods to cure his patient.

The cross shrine
The cross shrine is prepared. Three crosses have pine branches attached to them. Red geraniums are tied at the intersection of the cross. A layer of pine needles is strewn in front of the shrine. Incense is lit. Then a drinking ritual. A drink-pourer pours rum into shot glasses, hands them to the men in order of seniority. Music is then played.

Five sacred mountains
A view of the five mountains within the ceremonial centre at Zinacantan. A woman moves mountains. (Animation)

Sweetened squash
For nine days ritualists gather each morning outside the church of San Lorenzo and eat sweetened squash to commemorate the nine months of the Virgin's pregnancy.

Face of the maize
A Tzotzil curing ceremony in which the shaman throws maize grains to determine how many parts of the inner soul are missing in cases of soul-loss.

It was freezing. Nerida dragged the hissing kerosene heater closer to the bed, and burrowed under the quilt. She wrote a covering letter to Juana, explaining that she would place herself in Juana's hands regarding the outcome of the footage. She dropped the pages into the cardboard box at her feet, which contained numerous canisters of exposed film she would deliver to Mexico City. After taping the box closed, she lay back on the bed listening to the *merengue* playing remotely on the stereo in the *sala*. Alexis and Drusilla chose the same records over and over. It was a relief when they stopped.

I have always been a good girl, Nerida said to herself, as she nested in the bed. I have swayed with the wind. Because it's a sugar-rush, it's marzipan, that eruption between the legs, and also on the nape of the neck, and your breasts, cupped, and your arms gripped so hard the bruises remain to jerk off your memory, and it's powerful. It's very important. But it doesn't make up for being the complement of a sentence and not its subject.

24

Nerida ran down the flight of stairs into the *sala*, her body slanted forward with the impetus of primitive energy. She leapt the last three steps lightly, freed from the great coils of sluggish things that had been squeezing her brain for a long time, trying slowly to crush her. She had gathered her strength and thrown off the asphyxiating creature. Drusilla reclined, her black dress set off nicely by the bright striped blankets covering the couch, looking decadently stagey, a magazine held in her hand, the image of stasis. There was no progression with these people. They spun in circles.

Drusilla looked up, beautifully, as Nerida passed in front of the cavernous hearth.

'Hi, Drusilla. Suddenly you're here. I'd lost sight of you.' A cold draught sneaked around Nerida's legs.

'Where are you going?'

'To see Alexis. He needs a break.'

'I'm waiting for him to finish, too. Then we are going to have lunch.'

Nerida did not believe her. She was grateful for the good manners that had been hammered into Drusilla from birth. They prevented the sister from forcibly restraining Nerida, which she saw Drusilla longed to do since there was no other tactic left.

'Leave him alone,' Drusilla said softly – and then, when Nerida continued to move towards the office door, 'Do you have any idea what despair he must have felt when he was cured of his seizures? There was nothing exceptional there any more.'

'I was living with him. I know everything about his despair.'

Drusilla allowed herself an arctic smile. She dropped her magazine. 'Really? I think you're just a little girl who likes to fuck.'

Nerida stood still and regarded Drusilla for a few seconds. 'That's exactly it,' she said. 'I like to fuck Alexis. I don't want to dominate him or cast a spell or take his photograph. I want to get in the car with him and drive away and buy groceries on the other side of the border. So you – you can stop playing in our backyard now. Haven't you got a home to go to?'

Drusilla was so angry her hands were trembling, but there was something else behind her fury, something that kept the smile fixed on her face, something she knew that caused Nerida to feel uneasy. Nerida made herself dismiss the tremor of disquiet by reminding herself that Drusilla specialised in complications. She said out loud, 'We're not epic, you know. We're just two girls having a spat.'

Turning away, Nerida entered Toos's office without knocking. Alexis was bent over the typewriter, his shoulder-blades protruding sharply through his cotton shirt. The remnants of Drusilla's influence were heard through the door – the *merengue* record, manically upbeat.

'Alexis.' Nerida's fingers skimmed the crown of his head. 'I'd like you to stop now.'

Alexis frowned at the sheet of paper in front of him. 'Oktar Zich,' he said, studying Nerida through hooded, suspicious eyes, 'who was Hostinsky's successor at the Caroline University, he threw out the whole idea of Herbartian formalism. Incredibly, he thought of aesthetic phenomena as psychic. The Czechs knew about this a long time ago.

I think it's possible. I think a supernatural shimmer is possible.'

'I'd like you to stop, baby. We have things to do. We have to pack. We have used up our time here.'

'I'm working.'

'It'll wait.'

'I'm working on something very *vital*.'

Nerida began massaging his shoulders, which were gristly with tension. 'It's pointless to repeat lamentations, to dance backwards, to abstract yourself to the point of extinction. Got to get back your sense of humour. Nothing makes us laugh here, except in a gallows kind of way.'

Alexis ceased typing but made no other response to Nerida's kneading fingers. So, clasping his wrist, she towed him to the day-bed. He lay down. She placed her fingers hard around his lips, caging his mouth, and sucked out his tongue and kissed him for a long time. She pulled off her pants, hiked up her skirt, knelt over him. He raised his hands and his fingertips stroked the top of her thighs. He stroked her for minutes, repetitively, until she began to ache.

'Alexis,' she said, 'it's true. I am a girl who likes to fuck, but only with you. It's important. And at the moment, it's all that's left of you.'

She thought: Sex – you – imitates the sublime while at the same time hiding in caves.

She dropped forward so that she was leaning over him like a canopy, so that he could run his tongue through her hair and into the slippery slit and thrust it in. He was helpless. She would only let him use his mouth.

She thought: Sex – which is you because you are my cock – is exquisite because it is truthful. It is a marble plinth sunk in a swamp and engraved with fine exhortations that you cannot read at a distance. To get close enough to make out

220

the inscription, you have to get your feet dirty. You have to wade and flounder.

Sex is a neurological incision.

It's a stringed instrument, it's a racquet, 3,000 lbs. per square inch. She removed his clothes.

Sex causes loss of weight; then inflames the appetite causing large meals to be consumed.

Sex is not the façade of the building.

After undressing him, she tied him to the day-bed using her belt and scarf so that he was immobilised. He made a cramped X.

'You can't do anything,' she whispered. 'You can't make decisions. You can't act. All you can do is place yourself in my hands. You are at my disposal and I would like you to wait now, because you have made me wait, wondering what will become of us.'

Nerida stood up and let her skirt fall. She left the room. When she entered the kitchen, Drusilla was standing at the stove making hot chocolate while Graciela plucked a chicken. Neither woman spoke to Nerida. She opened the pantry door and after removing half a dozen eggs, took two bowls from a shelf and began to separate the eggs, the whites in one, the yolks in the other. Still Drusilla and Graciela said nothing. Nerida picked up the bowl of viscous egg-whites and carefully carried it away.

In the bedroom she dipped her fingers in the albumen and began to lubricate Alexis's penis. It pulsed and bucked like a small animal. He moaned and said, the first words he had spoken since he had been consigned to the day-bed, 'I can't look in your face.'

Nerida released him from his bonds and throwing off her clothes, lay down next to him, on her stomach on the floor. 'Then you can do it from behind. Use the stuff in the bowl.'

221

Alexis dripped the egg-white into the crack between her buttocks, and she was delighted that he was acting. She was not interested in experiencing an orgasm. She simply wanted him to focus on something that was sensational and dirty and nothing to do with words and everything to do with her but at a remove. He fucked her and fucked her until he came. The semen dripped down between her legs.

They lay silently in one another's arms for a long time. Eventually Nerida turned to kiss him, but he shunned her with a sharp, 'Don't!' She thought she had entranced him, but now he got up briskly, dressed, and left the room.

Nerida twisted into her clothes. She would let him sleep and then they would strap the wings on their ankles and fuck off out of there. She touched the typewriter in an absurd demonstration of affection and touched his notebook. His manuscript. A silly surge of love, despite everything, made her want to moon over his words. She opened up the pages and read:

When I was nine I began to accompany my father to the lowlands. My sister, at the same age, was required to become useful in the house. Until then we had gambolled in the privileges of childhood, having enjoyed unconditional affection and been given toys with which to amuse ourselves. It took some time for us to realise that a drastic change had taken place; that we were now expected to follow orders.

Naturally, we preferred to return to a time when we were exempt from obligation to others, when, even though we were small, our selves filled up the entire house.

In the normal course of events, this reversion would not have been possible. But one day I was struck by lightning and our circumstances were altered. All the power in our parents was diverted to me. They dimmed and I shone. My sister, who was my natural ally, fused herself to me in order to overcome the separation that happened to women.

We grew older. My sister, who was more tightly bound than I, refused to listen when petitioners, potential lovers, came to the house. Outside in the darkness they shouted for a jug of rum or a sharp axe or anything at all to get the door open. According to custom, these nominal requests would be granted and in that way the house would be breached, and the father would give in. But this did not happen. My sister shunned the nets of fruit and the smaller gifts of maize and tortillas and, as the rest of us unaccountably languished, there was no one to disagree with her.

She was determined to cause a scandal so that we would be free of petitioners and their trials of courtship. Because she was my sister I wanted to help her and this I could do because I knew the words to use. Therefore I also understood the power of omission that leads another into sin.

Nerida tore her eyes from the page. She did not recognise this chronic voice as Alexis's voice, but having banged up against an overgrown monolith on an uninhabited moor, she felt injured. She turned over sheets and sheets of words. What she read caused her grief:

I knew I had ruined her and ruined myself. But that our punishments would be separate and according to our cultures. The male members of her family perceived her violation to be a slur on their honour. Pleasure was not permitted in her life. By that I don't mean the banality of orgasm, I mean even the meanest example of autonomy. She was contracted by birth to breed and gather firewood and make tortillas. I have no sensitivity towards the axioms of the tribe. I was interested in exploding sensitivity, since it seemed to be so selective in its sensitivity. I was hot for *mano a mano*. I believed that they would come after me and clash in the flesh as opposed to a pale accounting written on the Eastern seaboard of the United States, hiding in the fort of the university. But they struck at her because she was the weaker. Because she was there.

She should have been sleeping. But she walked to the pine tree, which was still threaded with geraniums, and waited for her older brother to exact his countenanced vengeance. He, like me, was deranged. No logic applied, except for the reductive demands of machismo. It is neither colourful nor charming but it is as ballistic as a meteorite. We continue to be excited by blood.

What are the sins against hope?

The sins against hope are despair and presumption.

What is presumption?

Presumption is a foolish expectation of salvation without making use of the means necessary to obtain it.

The inhabitants of Xul Vo remained silent, although they must have heard her screams. Petul hurled at her with his machete. His aim was to decapitate her and throw her body over a cliff. Nothing would be said. Everyone would agree it was a private matter and besides, Petul's reputation would be inflated. A man who murders is a man who murders. He commands respect and respect is respect no matter how craven. At the last moment, when the machete began its thin, whippy descent, she threw herself aside. Because she was a refusnik and that was why I had been drawn to her. She would not make the tortillas. She would not be killed. But she was slashed. Her forearm, which she raised to fend him off. The backs of her thighs, where his machete cut through her skirt as she ran. Her hair, her braids, which he seized as she fell and sliced off because she did not deserve to possess the attributes of a woman, which maddened men no matter what she did and served as an expression of the endemic rancour of her menfolk. She had already refused a bridegroom; therefore she did not deserve to live. She kicked him in the balls and outran him, because she was fit. She knew how to run. She ran, bleeding, without crying out because who would come to her rescue?

Her violator called out the brothers in a moment of disgusting *de facto* chivalry. Chivalry was always corrupt. And he could not believe it when they dropped their machetes at the sight of him. He was not Zinacantan. He did not exist.

She was bandaged in the *ladino* clinic, refusing to utter a word. They shrugged and said, it is a private matter. She was returned to her village where they said she would grow old for nothing. There is a verb in Tzotzil which means to talk to a woman is the same thing as having sex with her. This is joined with the articles of faith of the church.

What qualities must all sorrow have to obtain pardon from sin?

Sorrow for sin must have these four qualities: it must be true sorrow of the heart; it must spring from a supernatural motive; it must extend to all mortal sins committed; it must regard sin as the greatest of all evils.

How can we acquire true sorrow for our sins?

We can acquire true sorrow for our sins by thinking of the loss of heaven and the torments of hell.

Nerida laid the notebook, as if it were made of eggshells, delicately on the desk. Dozens of incendiary questions were laying waste to her mind. Placing her faith in the solidity of small, verifiable actions, she opened the wooden door and mounted the wooden staircase. She noted the yellowed plastered walls and the threadbare, excellent-ancient-example-of-something

225

runner sprawled the length of the corridor that led to the bedroom and another carved door. Who crafted these things? In the bedroom, the same white cotton quilt lay on the massive, dour bed and leaning against the window, there was a man she had known very well, his hands in fists on his hips.

'You're not sleeping,' she said redundantly.

Alexis shook his head. His hair had grown very long. It collapsed lankly behind his ears, was intersected by the nape of his neck and concluded just above his collarbone. He straightened and slipped his hands into his pockets and walked towards her, then halted just beyond arm's reach.

'Alexis. I can't stay in this house for another moment.'

'I am waiting for Eugene,' he said quietly. Removing a hand from one of his pockets, he began to tap his fingertips regularly on the bed-end. The tapping sounded hard and hollow like a horse galloping over sun-fired clay paddocks.

'I read something at your desk – I think it's about Xunka.'

The tapping ceased, with a jerk.

'Is it true? I don't ask on my own account. This is not a domestic accusation. What have you done?'

Reaching out a shaking hand, he hooked his fingers around the belt encircling her waist. She had used that belt half an hour ago in the belief that she was the panacea. The sugar-pill.

A car slithered up the driveway. A door slammed. The front door slammed, and Alexis's hand fell away.

'You'll hear,' he said. His voice was dull and slow, like somebody drunk.

They could hear Eugene shouting Alexis's name from the *sala*.

Alexis picked Nerida up, dumped her on the bed and wrapped the quilt around her tightly, clamping it close over her ears. 'Don't move!'

He left the room, but even with the door closed, ·Nerida could hear the rumbling avalanche of an argument below. She recalled the morning she had hugged the pillow in her bed, listening to her father call her mother's name, finally. She lay in the bed for an age, staring at the cardboard box containing exposed film and at the suitcases on top of the wardrobe. After the car accelerated angrily and sped away, there was still a long hiatus before Alexis pushed open the bedroom door. He was carrying a tape recorder, which he put on the floor.

'I want you to listen to this,' he said, 'and then say whatever you want. There's been a disturbance in the classroom. Eugene's subjects have withdrawn. No one wants to talk to him any more because I have brought them trouble. He went to the market and spoke to a man called Antun whose son was in a cornfield last week hunting birds.' Alexis rested against the dressing table and said, using a crazy impersonal tone, 'I was interested in suffering.'

He switched on the tape. A man spoke in Tzotzil for several minutes, his voice rising with indignation. Anyone listening to these hammering sentences could tell it was a bad story. Nerida said nothing, but she drew her knees up to her chest and embraced herself. Alexis stopped the tape.

'When Antun's son was in the cornfield,' he translated, 'they saw a man. They thought he was a spook. They saw the spook and Xunka in the cornfield and they had seen them one time before that, in the forest, although on that occasion they could not see what was happening. This time they saw the spook and Xunka in the cornfield, kissing. They saw them screwing. I don't know how they came to be screwing. Xunka is a girl with a dirty reputation and now she has passed it on to her family. The spook took off. They said he flew away using his winged sandals. Xunka's eldest brother, Petul, wanted to punish her. She should have sat with her shawl drawn over

227

her mouth. Whatever happens, it won't be dealt with by the *ladino* authorities. Everyone has agreed it is a private matter and for that reason they will no longer talk to Eugene. Antun says, the spook, he will grow old for nothing.'

Alexis looked at Nerida lying like a child under the quilt. She was an endless and blue lake. He had knelt at her side and ignored the echo of her voice.

'So she was punished. Petul cut her with a machete.'

Nerida felt a surge of nausea. Every organ in her shrank.

'He didn't manage to kill her. He was too drunk. Toos has gone to the hospital.'

'What I read . . . when was that written?'

'Before anything happened. But I knew it would happen.'

'That girl was horribly injured. Did you engineer that for your book?'

'Eugene doesn't care about her, after all. He's incensed because his work here has been corrupted by real events. By real fucking sex and blood but I say it's nothing to do with the infections and the declensions!'

'Stop.' Nerida held up her hand to ward off something threatening. A spook.

Alexis cried, 'I can only remember driving on a white road!'

Nerida retreated to the far side of the bed so that he could not touch her. 'Maybe you are mad, Alexis. I don't know. Maybe you are one of those mad geniuses. But I have this really simple desire to be simple. I can't get over . . . Jesus! She was attacked by animals! What is the point of all your education? What is the point of all these books? Go away. Far away.'

Nerida drew a circle around herself by force of feeling and seeing he could not enter it, Alexis left the room.

For some time Alexis walked automatically around and around the well while reality melted away all the elaborate images that had grown in his mind like crystals in a cave, secretly and inevitably. He had grown too large to throw himself into the well. He was left with vomitous consequences. A man's got to stand up for his crime.

A woman's voice called his name.

His sister took his arm and made him sit down on the coarse grass but that did not stop his agitation. She was speaking softly to him but he had to stand up again. A man lying down like a child, that was not right. A man walking round like an animal in a corral – that was not right either.

'You are ill,' Drusilla murmured, 'it was not your fault. Listen. The *agente* will be paid to see your story and then I'm going to see that you get help.'

She looked into his eyes and Alexis flinched at seeing pleasure, *schadenfreude*, there. Brushing hair out of his eyes she said, 'A sister is lifelong, Alexis. I'll take care of you.'

'Why didn't you hit me hard and stop me?'

'I'd never hurt you.'

'I have to see the *agente* myself,' and added when she shook her head, 'You want me to stay disgusted?'

'The point is to be practical.'

Gently, Alexis removed her hand from the vicinity of his face. 'What about Nerida?'

'She has discovered her own interests. She should pursue them.'

'Don't you think it's hard to find love? Harder than you think?'

Drusilla embraced him, lodging her head against his shoulder. He ought to have felt comforted, but her clasp induced in Alexis a feeling of suffocation and a strong desire to be free of her. He had been caught in Drusilla's loop all his life whether she was present or not. He was choosing the words that would extract her when Drusilla, perceiving his refusal,

229

stepped back and aimed an oxyacetylene gaze at him. 'Don't say anything about anything. But you must come with me. Please.'

Her gaze no longer had the power, in Alexis's eyes, to burn him down.

'I'm sick and fucked up,' he said, 'and staying with you will only make it worse. You can't speak for me or arrange my fate. I can't talk any more. I have to see Nerida.'

Alexis wanted to leave Drusilla with the knowledge that he did love her, but he knew that she would take that statement and turn it into a dangerous admission. She was an arsenal of rage. Any gesture he might have offered to assuage her isolation was pre-empted by the triumphant note in her voice as she said, 'You've missed that boat. She's gone. There's nothing there and you can't even see it. You never were all that clever. You only did what you were told.'

Alexis turned his back on her. Drusilla did not move as she watched him slither down the grassy slope and disappear through the arch into the courtyard. Tears, although she hated them, forced themselves into her eyes and spilled down her face. She examined the stupidly precious rings on her fingers and ground her teeth and cast around wildly in her mind for someone to punish but everyone, father, mother, brother, had escaped, leaving her stranded in the unbearable present.

Alexis saw at once that Nerida's suitcase was gone. And those cardboard cartons that he had forgotten to enquire about. *What had she been doing all this time?* Raúl, gravely, told him that she had taken a taxi, despite the expense. Alexis called the gallery, and after fielding Toos's concerned comments that danced around his idiocy, ascertained that Nerida was not there. And now Toos became genuinely concerned. 'Oh

230

no,' she breathed. 'She does not like to fly. The bus station. I will go there.'

'No.' said Alexis. 'It has to be me.'

She had not said goodbye to anyone. She had sat for an hour on a hard bench with her suitcase and her cardboard cartons at the bus station in San Cristóbal. But by the time Alexis screeched to a halt in the Dodge, parking in the middle of the street, Nerida was hurtling over the Sierra Madre in sheets of rain, visibility nil.

25

Nerida took one photograph, from the road, of the house where she had grown up and then returned to her car. The house had been painted a peachy colour. Three children on horseback turned into the gateway and trotted up the long driveway. Nerida was glad to see that there was more than one child. When she turned on to the highway, she saw that clouds were piled thousands of metres high. She was driving through a small country but it appeared to be limitless. On the car radio a woman sang, *Sadder light of love . . .*

When you looked closely, every detail was absorbing. To her left, a choked-up riverbed ran parallel to the road. Just south of Kawakawa, she passed alternately along the spines of ridges, with views of farmland, and through shadowy dips in the road, between screens of gorse and tea tree. Dairy factory followed sawmill on the twisting road and still the clouds were huge, like frozen tsunami. Entering Kamo, she stopped at a traffic light. This land was occupied by people whose names she didn't know. They ate fast food and lingered before shop windows that were dense with coloured texts. Even in the middle of nowhere, there was something going on.

Happy Dragon Chinese Takeaways.
Kamo Motel. Hot spa pool. Vacancy.
Houses swarmed over the hills outside Whangarei.
Auckland 169 km.
Fruit and veges. Drive in.

Drive in Honey. Hundred metre.
Boat ramp.
Between the hills, channels of brown water snaked into grey-green mangroves, mangroves for miles, and mud. Cows with rich coats grazed on low boggy land. Beneath a conga line of electricity pylons, sheep littered the hills.
Te Hana Nurseries. Wholesale citrus.
Bag your own Granny Smith.
Innumerable trees sent their long narrow shadows across the road. Between the trunks more vegetation pressed towards the frontier of tarseal. Nerida believed that she had never looked properly at anything before.
!Washout!
Slow down. Sheepworld and Campavan Park 200 m.
Auckland via Albany.
Windbreaks of supple, shivering poplars. Sheep-speckled paddocks fringed by Phoenix palms. Three white crosses rising from a ditch. Four windmills silhouetted on a ridge.
Puppies For Sale.
Increasing numbers of vehicles joined Nerida's surge towards the city. Cars hauling horse floats, boats or trailers. Wherever she looked, houses occupied the land and she felt the hum around her of inhabitants and activity. Cresting a hill, she was confronted by a clutch of tall, blunt buildings rearing from the far shoreline of Auckland's large and splendid harbour.
Bridge lanes open 1234 XXX.
As the sun fell beneath the horizon, Nerida drove at the bridge until she was soaring above the water, the masts of yachts everywhere sticking up out of the water like aerial mangrove roots. Before her lay a large, excited city, blazing with lights.

Nerida placed a bundle of stiff spaghetti upright in the saucepan of boiling water. As she took her hand away, the spaghetti splayed into disorder and then, under the influence of the rolling boil, became entangled. She thought: This disorder still contains the original pattern even though it is now broken. The perfection is always there, even if only by implication. It's just that it remains hidden. We yearn for a state of calm assurance, we yearn for invariance, for a strong force.

When the patient was asleep, needles were passed through his cheeks – their progress observed on the image intensifier that revealed the contents of his head – until they penetrated the skull. Once the needles were secure, two electrodes were threaded through the base of the brain. The patient's hair was not shaved. A nurse parted it in neat sections so that a further twenty-four electrodes, twelve on each side, could be attached using a glue gun.

Alexis woke with a pulsating toothache, which he had been told would be a side-effect of the procedure. He walked along the corridor to the day-room and back again, ceaselessly, with a machine strapped to his belt that would alert his observers to the onset of a fit. When he was tired of walking, he sat cross-legged on the bed, working over the final chapter of *Seizure*, which was turning out to be everything he had unconsciously aimed for: a self-administered, public rebuke. His publisher loved it. Alexis looked into the large mirror fitted into the wall opposite his complicated hospital bed, and waved.

Around 10 p.m. he fell asleep but his nurses, sitting sentry beside the infra-red video monitor, continued to observe him through the two-way mirror. At 2 a.m. Alexis threw back the covers. The neurophysiologist behind the glass smiled with satisfaction as the left Foramen Ovale electrode began to spike, like endless lightning.

'His aura has come on,' he said.

Alexis was on his feet, making an important point: 'Sssssss – psychic is revol-revulsanet-revol-revolution dead end. PLACES WE HAVE BEEN! Pl-pl-pl-places. Placemats. Place-channels not visions WHERE we are going.' His speech degenerated until he became completely nonsensical, speaking the electrical language of epilepsy.

Having established that Alexis's fits did indeed originate in the temporal lobes, his Californian doctors then apprised him of the Wada Test, which would confirm whether it was safe to perform an operation. Further indignities occurred. After they had buried a catheter in his groin, they introduced an anaesthetic that tracked up the left carotid artery – Paris! The mind-numbing suffocating kiss! The blur of neon – and knocked out the left half of his brain.

'Please raise your arms, Dr Serafin.'

His left arm reached for the ceiling. His right arm collapsed.

'OK, Dr Serafin,' said the neurophysiologist, who was armed with a clipboard. 'I would like you to name these objects.' He passed various images before Alexis's eyes.

'House. Car. Umbrella . . . Lipstick – sorry, that was a joke; rocket. I can tell you straight out that I've got a left anterior lobe focus of epilepsy. I've had it since I was a child.'

Alexis willingly submitted to these invasions since nothing could be worse than the grief he felt at losing Nerida. The neurosurgeon, a bronzed god replica, who had been honed and toned by his passion for surfing, as he confessed to Alexis after the Wada Test had been completed, drew an elongated, serrated shape on his notepaper and placed it before Alexis.

'This is the hippocampus. It lies under the temporal lobe. To guarantee a good result, we should remove it. It's part of the deep structure of the brain. If you don't take out the hippocampus, you don't get the deep structure. You don't solve the problem.'

'It's true. I've always had a problem with the deep structure.'

In the two and a half years since she had returned to New Zealand, Nerida had become practical. She lived in a roomy rented house in Auckland, filled with someone else's furniture, and earned her living as a freelance photographer. She was no longer glamorous, but it filled her with satisfaction to pay the electricity bill, to plant salad greens in the garden, and to teach sometimes at a polytechnic. It was an ordinary life. It was peaceful. Since she would always be in love with Alexis she was not agitated by loneliness. She did not enter the unnecessary torment of love-connections. She was autonomous.

It was strange to be home. Her accent didn't fit. People were sometimes disdainful of her portfolio because it was worldly. But the seasons made sense. You could see the weather happening in the west before it reached you. During the summer she walked on the shady side of the road and swam without having to make a long, irritating journey. The beach was accessible. Everything was accessible. You could grow roses side by side with fan palms. You could be private since in this society, intimacy was regarded with alarm, and you could be confessional, since intimacy was also desired.

Chopping chillis for the sauce, Nerida recollected polluted Mexico City and her eyes began to sting. She'd made a long, demanding bus journey, much of it through sheets of tears. In Mexico City, sleet had been falling from a sky the colour of oxtail soup. She had gone to Juana's house in the Zona Rosa with her cartons of footage and delivered them into Juana's hands with the hope that something could be created from them. And Juana had. She had hired Luz Perez to edit the footage into several short films which existed, in Mexico where they belonged, as a record of Indian life. And Nerida was happy about that.

With her back resting against the railings of the veranda, she ate the spaghetti from a large, shallow bowl. She was hungry. The last rays of the sun slanted through a variety of fruit trees in the garden, lighting up the leaves, inciting a shimmer. Before Nerida went to bed she massaged cleanser into her face, followed by a cool application of toner. Then the lemon scent of night cream. Taking care of herself. After the alarm woke her, she would eat a good breakfast and wave away regrets. Otherwise you might as well be incarcerated or dead. In the same way that a concert pianist daily exercises her fingers on the keyboard, Nerida maintained her sharpness of perception by every day pressing her eye to a viewfinder and shooting something, often the same object at different hours of the day or night – a white lace dress, for instance, glistening in its shroud of drycleaning plastic – since she was most of all absorbed by the play of light (those photons whose zero rest mass allowed them to travel infinitely far from deep space to her bedroom) and its capacity to alter anything it fell upon.

She'd read the reviews of Alexis's book *Seizure* which ended with his equivalent act of the *torero*, the goring and the pathetic dragging away of the beast with its entrails lagging behind – that is, the cutting of Xunka. But he had not spared himself. His shabby prosecution was also recorded. It could have been a private matter, he might have existed only in the annals of Zinacanteco gossip as a girl-thief, but he published everything. He was admired for his intellect and censured for his egotism. It was a brilliantly written description of a neurotic man who had succumbed to a criminal act because he could not sublimate his impulses by creating great works of art. A man who was not proud of himself. Nerida understood that the work was penitential.

He hadn't sent her a copy. Had famously retreated into anonymity.

She continued to dream about him. She washed her plate, placed it in the drainer and went out to the movies where people looked at her in the foyer and were captured, briefly, by her presence.

On a freezing, rain-struck morning in Oregon, a thick envelope was delivered to the facility known as Cascade House, which existed for the recuperation of burnt-out head-cases, a ghetto for the victims of tortured intellect. Ironically, as far as Alexis was concerned, although maybe it was fate – who the hell knew any more? – Cascade House was situated on the outskirts of the city of Eugene, which harboured the University of Oregon. Having written his self-damaging book, Alexis had incarcerated himself here, waiting for a transformation which he had decided he could not trust to surgery. His brain still contained a hippocampus, a sea-monster lurking in the depths, which he hoped to pacify by force of will rather than the scalpel. He had injured everyone. The last casualty had been Drusilla, who had quit San Cristóbal leaving no forwarding address. She could forgive the wounding of Xunka but she could not forgive Alexis's desire to live separately from her, and he could not pay the price she wanted to exact for her love. During the year he had passed at Cascade House, nothing had happened. No trance. No fit. No lunacy. In the autumn he had picked fruit and had not been bored. He tried to make a joke of it, Alexis Serafin picking apples, but all his smooth irony had evaporated along with the bad weather in his brain, and so he gave up constantly trying to position himself, and picked the apples. It was good exercise.

Returning from his habitual walk in the forest, which he especially appreciated in winter when it numbed his body,

Alexis stopped suddenly at the gate. The mailman was driving away. Alexis took a walk every day at this same time, precisely to avoid the arrival of the mail, which filled him alternately with dread and disappointment. He paused, nevertheless, at the pigeonholes, and found a large, thick envelope addressed to him.

Alexis's burnished wooden room deliberately emulated the simplicity of a cell, except that it was heated and the mattress was orthopaedic. He shook the contents of the envelope on to the pine desk. Inside the cover of the French quarterly *Quoi?*, pages of documentation invited him to register for A Conference Concerning Ethnomethodology to be held in Mexico City. It took Alexis at least ten minutes to absorb a brick of text – 'Ethnomethodology's member's language style, so often dismissed as "wilfully obscure" or "much ado about nothing" is really a member's Reconstructed Poetic functioning as a literary idiolect' – seemingly translated by an initiate enjoying a paroxysm at the feet of his guru.

The guru grinned from the cover of *Quoi?*. Eugene Rinehart had lost some hair, which emphasised his bulging forehead apparently packed with brains. He was wearing a striped poncho. Written across his concealed groin, in English, was the sentence: 'Making Strange: Rinehart's infamous interventions – total zero-zone of reality-imbedded meaning.'

Alexis sat down on the bed and read Eugene's article. Eugene claimed to be the progenitor of a new form of ethnographic description that spoke in an elliptical style notable for its repetition, tautology and personal interruptions, 'For are we not all ritualists and of central-concern?' He was, according to himself, 'a masked ninja medicine-man who preferred exhibitable acts of hands-on analysable surgery'. He was his own analysis. Having been the famous subject of an ethnographic study (see Alexis Serafin's *Seizure*), Eugene had become practically cosmological. His students filmed him in the field and they filmed him recording the conversations of surgeons as they performed an eye operation. ('Note here the appositeness of Rinehart's "revisioning" concern.')

Alexis gazed at the ceiling and smiled tiredly. Sometimes a man will do anything, even dress up as a masked ninja medicine-man, to fill up the entire house with his ego even though he spreads himself so thin he is in danger of bursting. Alexis could not argue with Eugene's appropriation of appropriation except to say that the road petered out in a desert and those who travelled there died for lack of sustenance.

His smile faded as he examined the conference schedule. Astonishment turned to outrage when he read that Eugene was to deliver a paper called 'Zatocoding and Surrealist Automatism in the Zinacanteco Films of Nerida Simmonds'.

'Oh yes,' said Juana, when Alexis phoned her, 'Eugene wishes to make something of this and I am happy about it. After all, he facilitated her situation.'

'He what?'

'He encouraged her. He suggested she make a visual record of subjects he was studying.'

'Juana, that's not true. I can't believe that Nerida would have told you that. It was her own work.'

'I didn't ask her about her motivation. Anyway, they weren't finished films, more a collection of footage, and when Eugene got in touch with me last year he put it all in context.'

'But he's using her,' Alexis protested. 'He's stealing her work.'

'It doesn't belong to her.' Juana insisted. 'It belongs to us. She gave it to us. This conference is a boost for the department here and, I have to say, a boost for Nerida if she needs the recognition. Eugene's internationally regarded now. I don't understand what you expect me to do.'

240

'I'm protesting because whatever Nerida shot was personal. The films she made are nothing to do with enhancing Eugene's reputation.'

'If she has a problem, then let her do the protesting. I have sent her, out of courtesy, a copy of the schedule but I haven't heard back from her. And that doesn't surprise me. This was stuff she wanted to leave behind.' There was a pause, then Juana said crisply, 'I don't know why you, of all people, should be so particular about ownership.'

Alexis could not reply to that. Instead, he asked Juana for Nerida's address.

He put down the phone and paced up and down in the front room of the sanitorium which was deliberately light and bright. The room was endless and blue like a lake and you knelt at its side and ignored the echo of your voice. Lie with me! Eventually, he could no longer stand the confinement, and strode outside into the snow-rain and climbed a track in the fir forest. The landscape of eastern Oregon was familiar. Timber. Volcanically induced lakes. A moody sea frottaging itself against hunching cliffs. Like home. Evergreen.

Dearest Nerida

How are you? How *are* you? Generally but most of all in particular? I would like to hear everything you have to say but I can't because I put an ocean between us. Where did I go for such a long time when I told you I would never leave you? I think my mind was like some fields burned off for planting. And then the clear sky is marred by a haze of smoke.

I'm not affected any more by that morbid letter.

I am no longer strange, although I'm very tired of being foreign.

I woke up before dawn and remembered your telling me how Stan Brakhage said how all the places in his early films had been destroyed, how almost all the people in the early films had disappeared or died. He saw some sinister interchange or imperceptible energy that could become destructive. Did you read that to me from your Schneemann book?

I think I have been released from that trigger because the letter Z is not adequate to my meaning. Nothing here and nowhere in this hemisphere is adequate to your meaning.

An hour has passed since I wrote the last paragraph. I write your name and there is nothing else. I've thought of many, many amusing strategies to get your attention, I've been bargaining with the English language to give me a break and deliver up the incantation. But I don't think you would be impressed.

I have to reach you.

I cannot live without you.

Please write.

I love you, I love you.

Alexis.

Nerida removed Alexis's letter from the box on a still morning. After reading it several times she put on a tape and cranked up the volume until the music was loud enough to make her feel like dancing. She did not reply. She was at ease in the house with work to occupy her and a sweet emotional song about somebody else's heartache flooding the living room. She didn't write back because she believed that a correspondence would lead to more introspection, of which she had had her fill, or to an exchange of cleverness. Alexis would make a joke about subcarpathian Russians and she'd counter with a reminiscence of an hysterical moment they had shared in a record shop on Oxford Street. They would write letters for a while which would be nothing but a sentimental, moribund courting expressed in hieroglyphics.

It wasn't enough to write. There was more than writing but she was not sure if Alexis would agree with that.

As she drove to an appointment with her students, Nerida sent Alexis a message, mentally. When she arrived in the classroom, she examined the photographic assignments. Some of these boys and girls fought fatal duels with themselves, looking for pretexts – the merest of slights, the extremity of chemically induced alienations – to wound their personalities. Nerida had many things to say on that subject, beginning with her perception that the *Zeitgeist* encouraged the expression of wanton tempers and a consequent lifelong affair with self-aggravation and blame.

With a lurch the Boeing began its descent, sinking rapidly towards the lights below. The change in air pressure muffled the ambient noise inside the plane. Alexis used his fingers to close his nostrils and exhaled forcefully until his ears popped and everything sounded normal again. For the first time in more than two years he felt light and sexual. He regarded the many tiny ten-point zeds repeated on the paper napkins and the walls of the cabin and scattered through the in-flight magazine. No sorcery emanated from them.

When he landed, it was almost midnight and he could not discern anything other than a large glowing neon sign that said: 'Auckland', which boldly announced his city, his home, his place. As he exited the automatic doors of the airport, he breathed in fragrant air. Gazing up at the sky, he recognised the constellations. Riding in a taxi to a motel near the airport, he recognised the foliage.

In his neutral motel room, Alexis placed his suitcase on a stand at the end of the bed, turned on the television and looked for Nerida's name in the phone book. He could not find it. Directory Service expressed regret on behalf of the communications network and thanked him for his enquiry.

243

Thrusting his right hand into his jacket pocket, he brought out the balled-up napkin he had been writing on as the plane lowered itself over Auckland. He could write out the sincere scribble in a fair hand and post it in the morning. He could write for some time, possibly decades, in a fair hand, a facsimile of action. Another plane roared overhead. Alexis called a taxi.

Travelling through empty streets, Alexis asked: Strange letter Z, is your name nemesis? I don't think so. I think you were the afterglow of recollection. I clung to the psychotic repetition of a pattern traced in childhood when the possibility of the beach was wiped out by my removal to more sophisticated locations. A man might have a permanent soul and an animal soul, but he felt whole again. It made no sense to say, here, rushing along these wide, naive streets, I am a girl-thief. It was true, he had loved himself, his reputation, his status, his definition to the exclusion of all else. He could have fallen in the pool and drowned. He could have grown old for nothing. But he had ceased travelling that path. The sedan in which he was riding turned slowly into a driveway and stopped. Alexis paid his fare, bade the driver good-night and climbed the steps to the veranda.

Nerida was dreaming. Of large white houses lining the streets of a hyperdimensional universe populated by moon-ballerinas who weren't scientific enough. She was knocking at their doors looking for the girls who were throwing a party. Someone knocking at the door. Nerida woke up. Someone knocking at her double-locked door.

When she had released the catches and saw Alexis framed in the doorway, she said, 'What made you come?'

'You. The strong force.'

Nerida sighed and numbly smoothed her hair. She was not sure if shattered things could be repaired. No one had yet come up with a satisfactory unifying theory. But she let him into the hall. His hair was flecked with grey. He was dragging a large suitcase, which she eyed, and said, 'This isn't a flying visit?'

'I'm sorry I'm so late.'

'Well – just get into the bed. Don't say anything. What can we say?'

Alexis undressed and crawled into her bed, which smelled of perfume and her body. She turned her back to him so that he could encapsulate her, in what had been their customary sleeping positions, and since they were both exhausted, they slept deeply without dreaming.

Around dawn when they woke simultaneously, Nerida adjusted herself inside his embrace. 'Move over,' she said, 'and give me some room.'

'Nerida,' he whispered, his hand lying lightly on her hip. He wished to slide his palm into the hollow of her waist and place his hand on the small of her back and pull her close but he did not want her to think that he was practising a seduction.

'What do you want?'

'You. I want to stay here with you.'

'My life here is small which means that I can understand it. I do small, finite things. It probably isn't big enough for you. I don't need the whole world any more. I don't know if I need you. You were disgustingly destructive. You thought you were heavenly. So fucking important.'

Alexis sat up. He was so tired he could sleep for a complete winter, here in this room. But he got to his feet because Nerida had left the bed. 'I'm not immutable. Could I just walk around your house?'

She nodded and brushed her hand across his shoulder in a move to steady herself. He could still send her into a spin and she loved that sensation, but she did not want to fall down.

He wanted to ask if she had read his book and understood that he had paid for his vanity, but that in itself was a vain question.

She said, 'I haven't read your book, but I think I know what it's about.'

Nerida stood under the shower letting the deluge of water melt her muscles while Alexis walked around her house and she thought about him walking around her rooms. He felt at home. Lying down again on her bed, he breathed her in. His lungs expanded. His limbs were warmed by a shaft of sunlight streaming through the sash window. For a long time he had been unable to rest. He had been seduced by unreal visions. And she had been passive. Then his brain became quiet.

When the splatter of water in the bathroom ceased, he got up and made the coffee while she was drying herself. He opened the window in the kitchen, and thought about her skin, and how he would like to kiss it. You love someone to overcome desolation of the soul. You think it's fleeting – cadence of voice, shadow of jawline, texture of hair, swipe of fingertips, shape of feet – but it's the solid land. You're so busy walking on it and building on it, you don't pay attention to it unless an earthquake strikes. All your acquisitions, your crystal glasses and your oil paintings, crash to the floor but you don't care about them any more. You would like the earth to stabilise. You realise you can live out in the open for however long it takes because you're so thankful to be alive.

This woman, he said aloud, as he flicked through the pages of her calendar to see what she had planned to do without him, can ask me for anything and I will do it.

Nerida entered the kitchen, with a towel wrapped around

246

her, and sniffed the aroma of coffee. Her face was translucently clean. Her hair hung in long dripping strands over her shoulders. She placed her hand against Alexis's cheek and leaned into him.

She asked, 'Will you give up the storm-tossed life?'

A NOTE ON THE AUTHOR

Debra Daley lives in Auckland with her two sons, where she works as a screen writer. *The Strange Letter Z* is her first novel.